Amazing Patterns Zen Doodle

Adult Coloring Book, Easy and Relaxing Coloring Pages For Meditation And Happiness

Volume 1

Contact : Rabieyou7@gmail,com

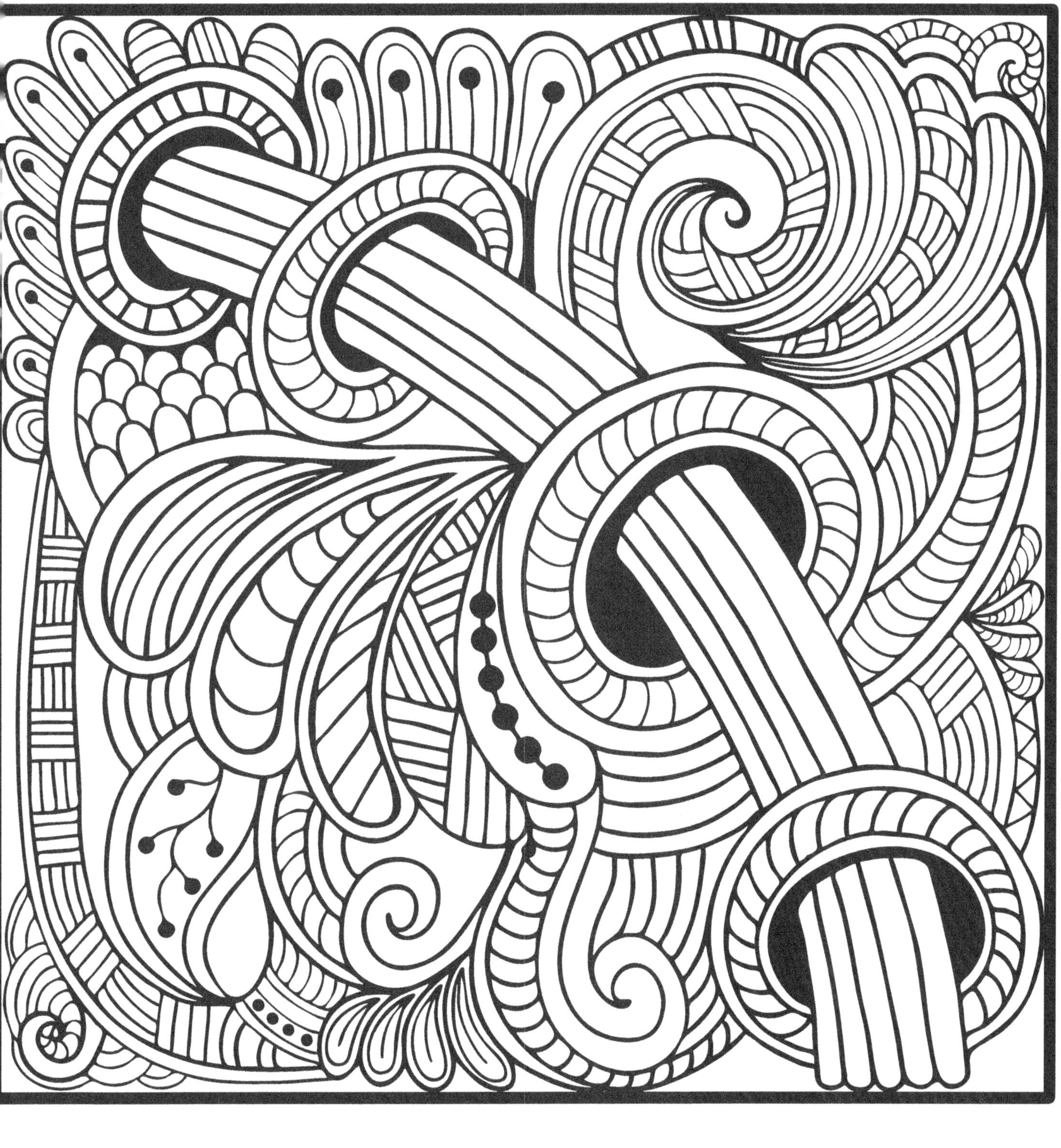

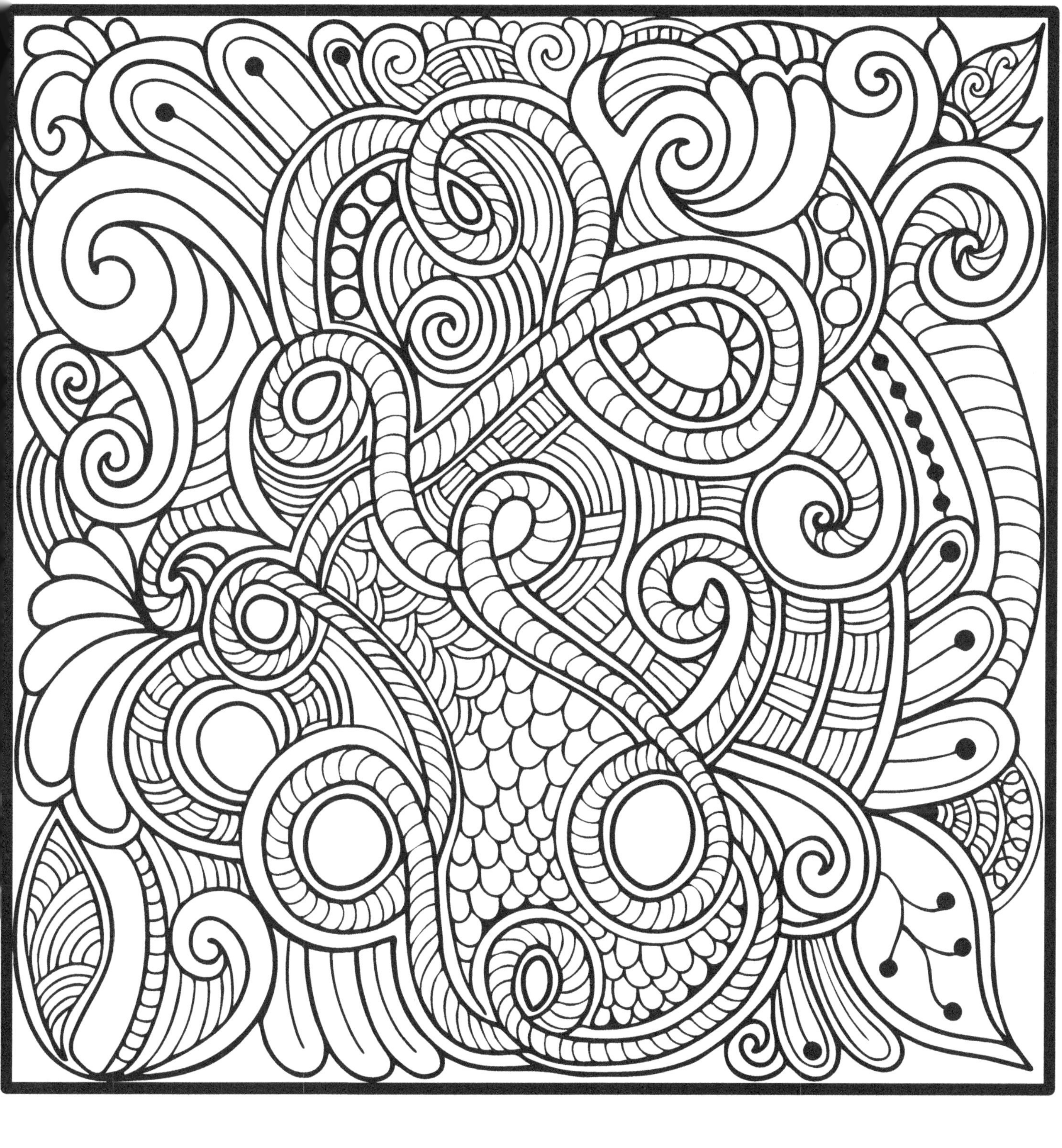

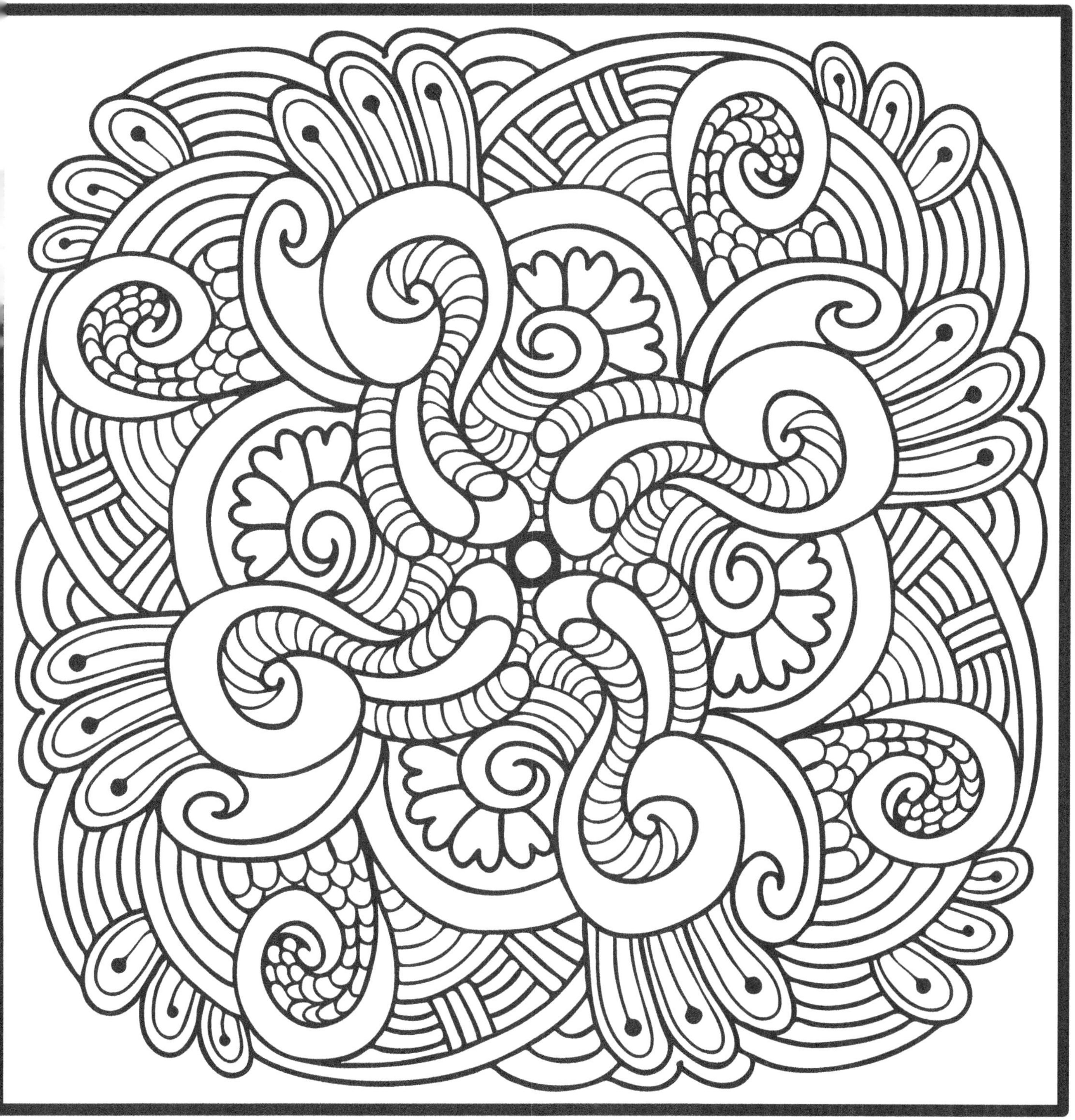

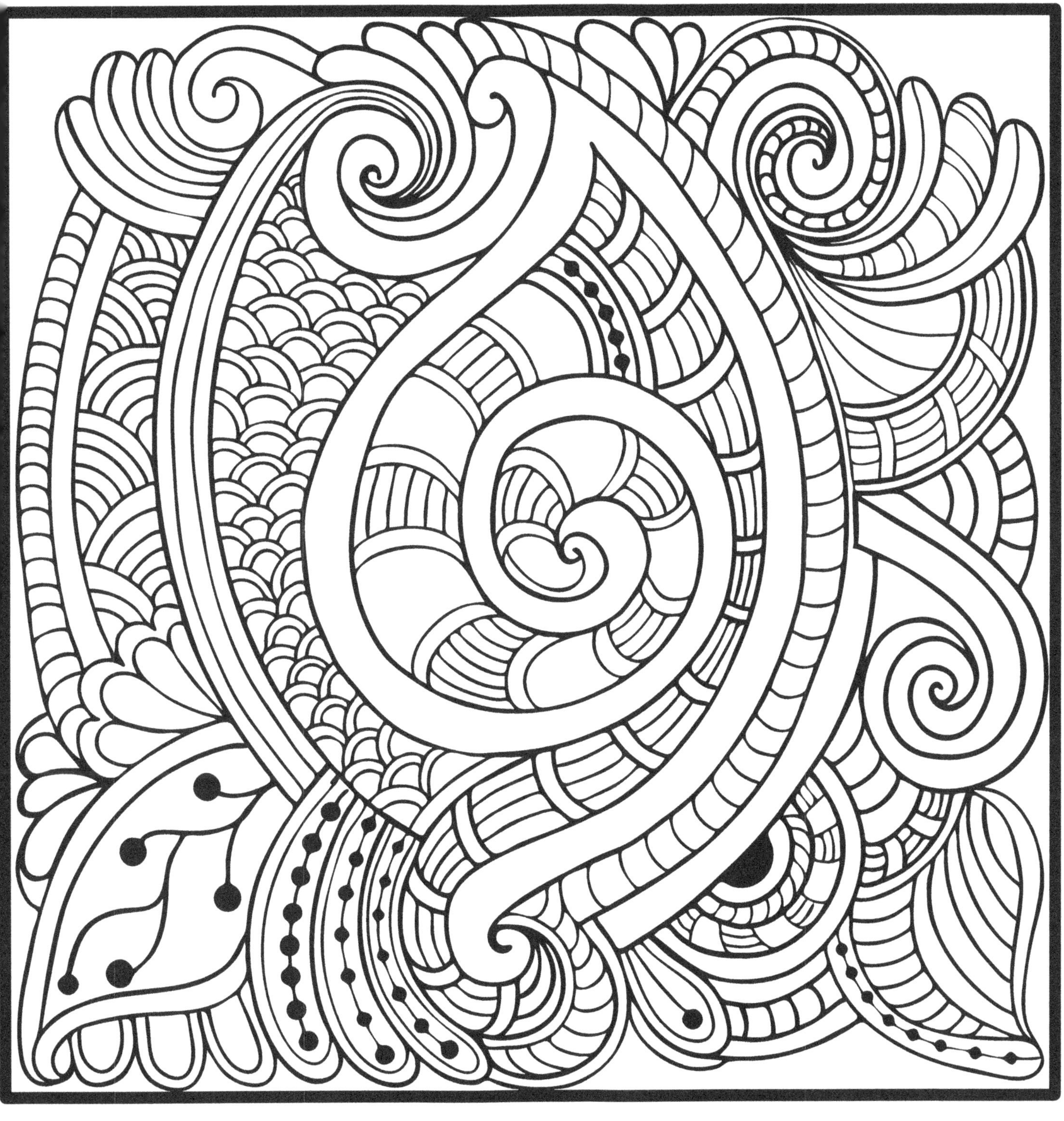

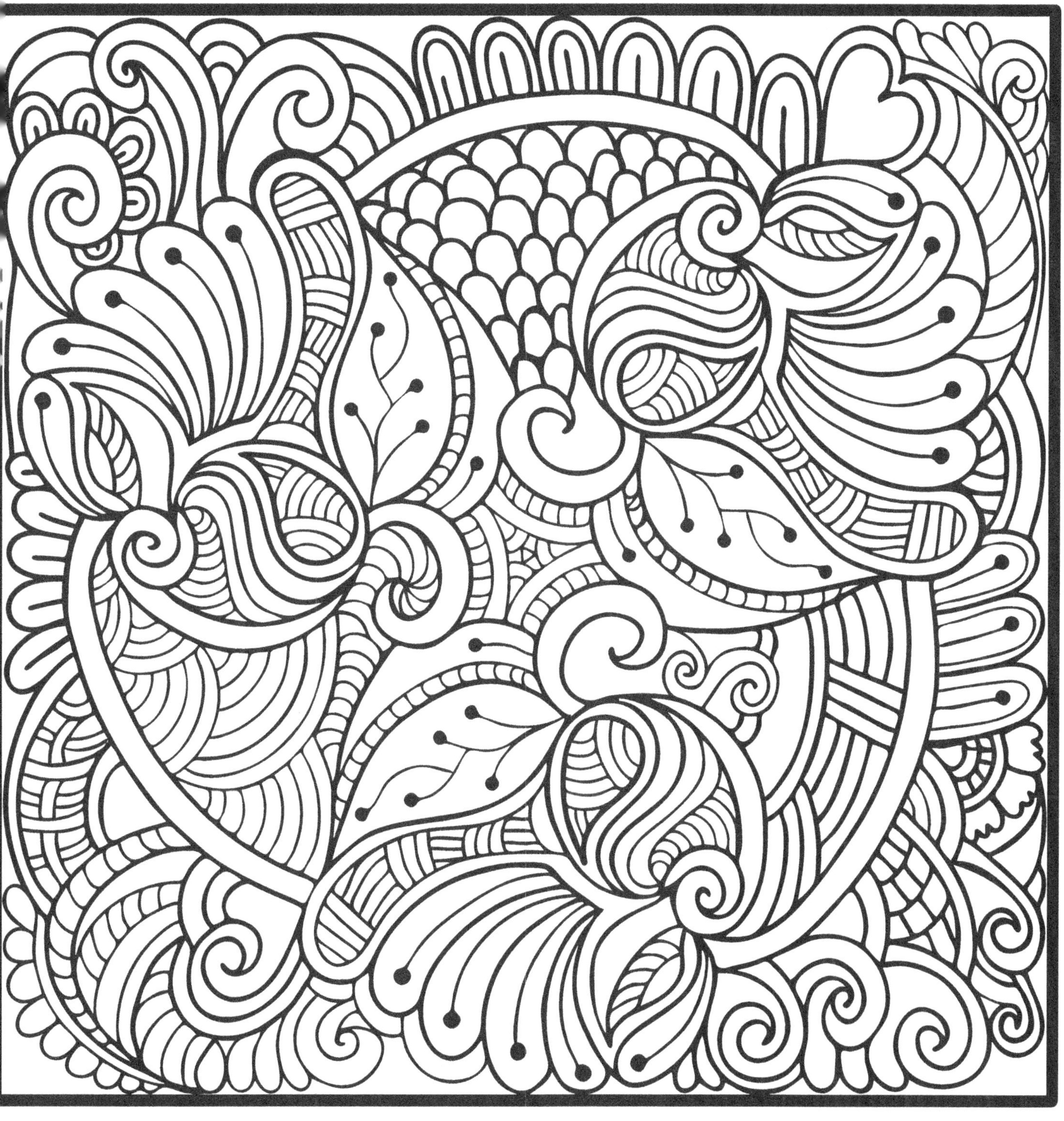

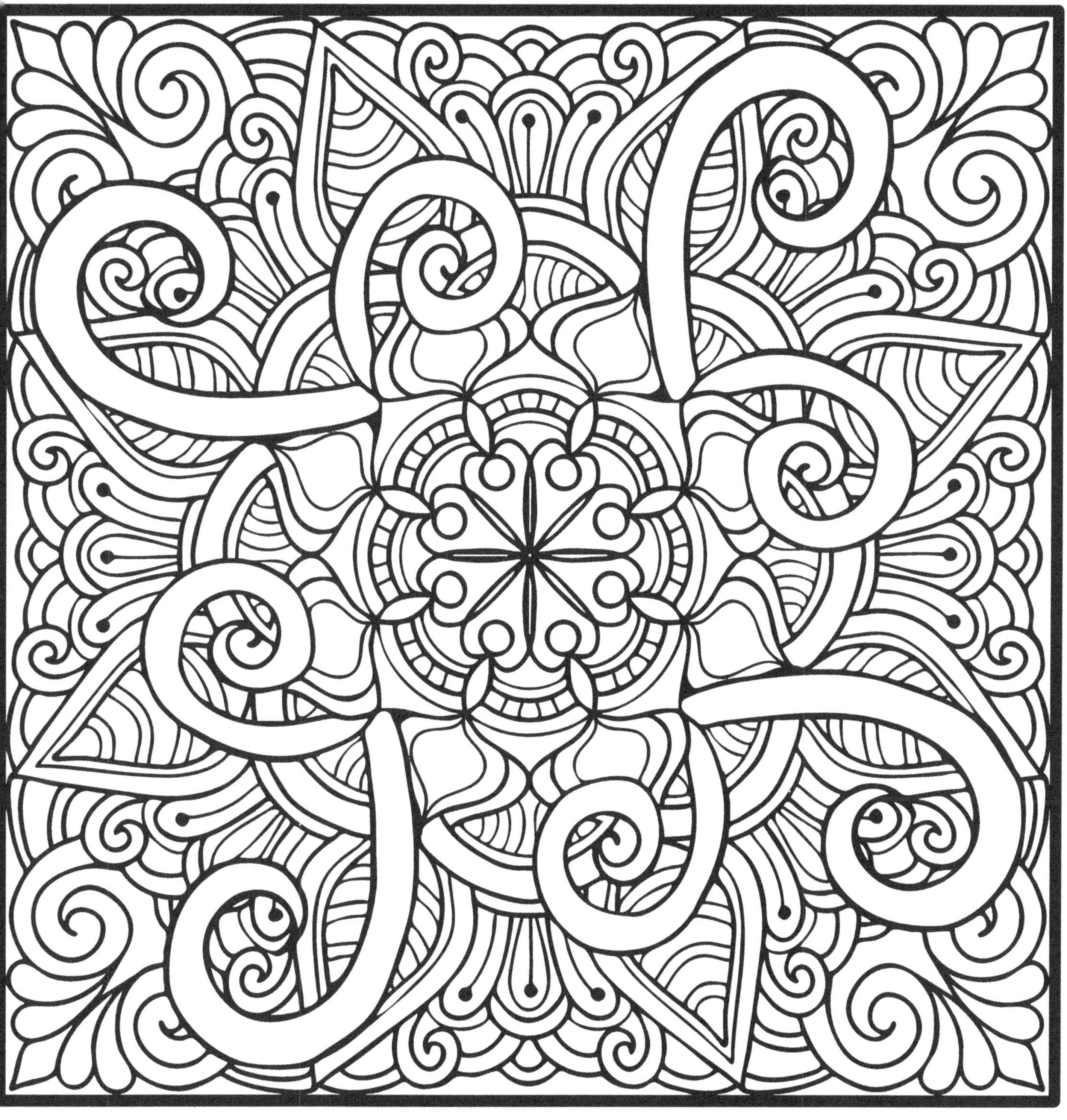

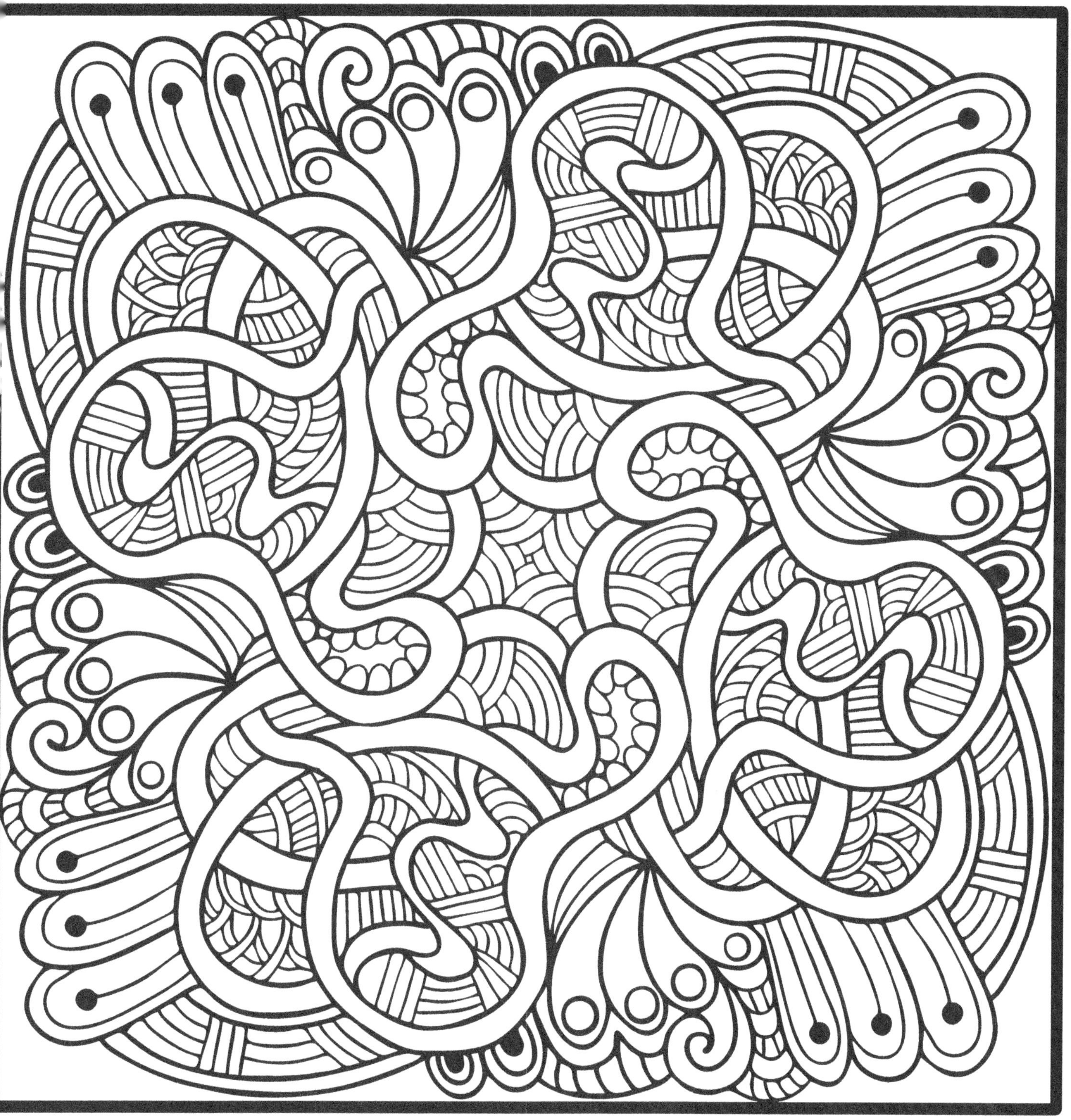

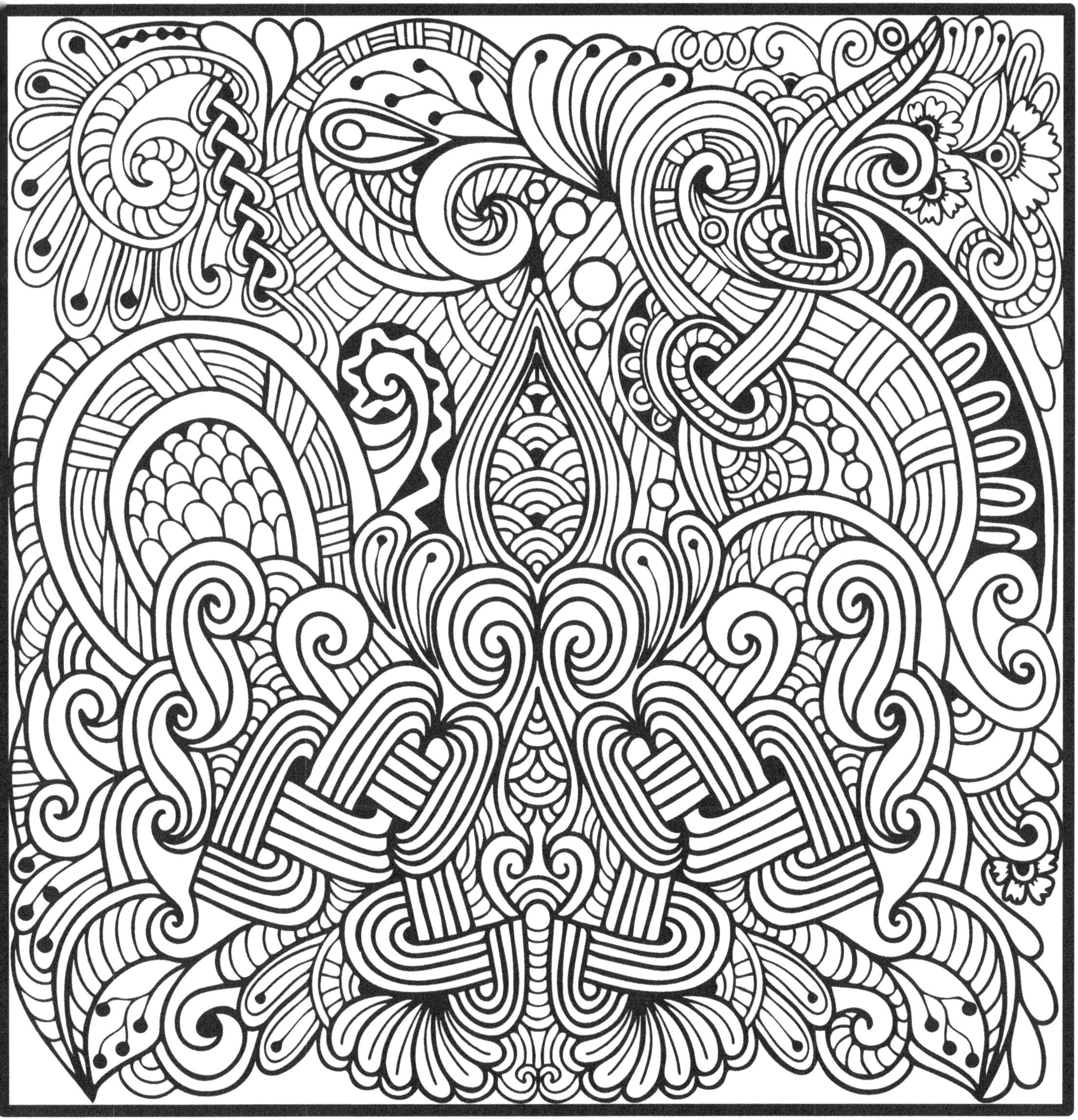

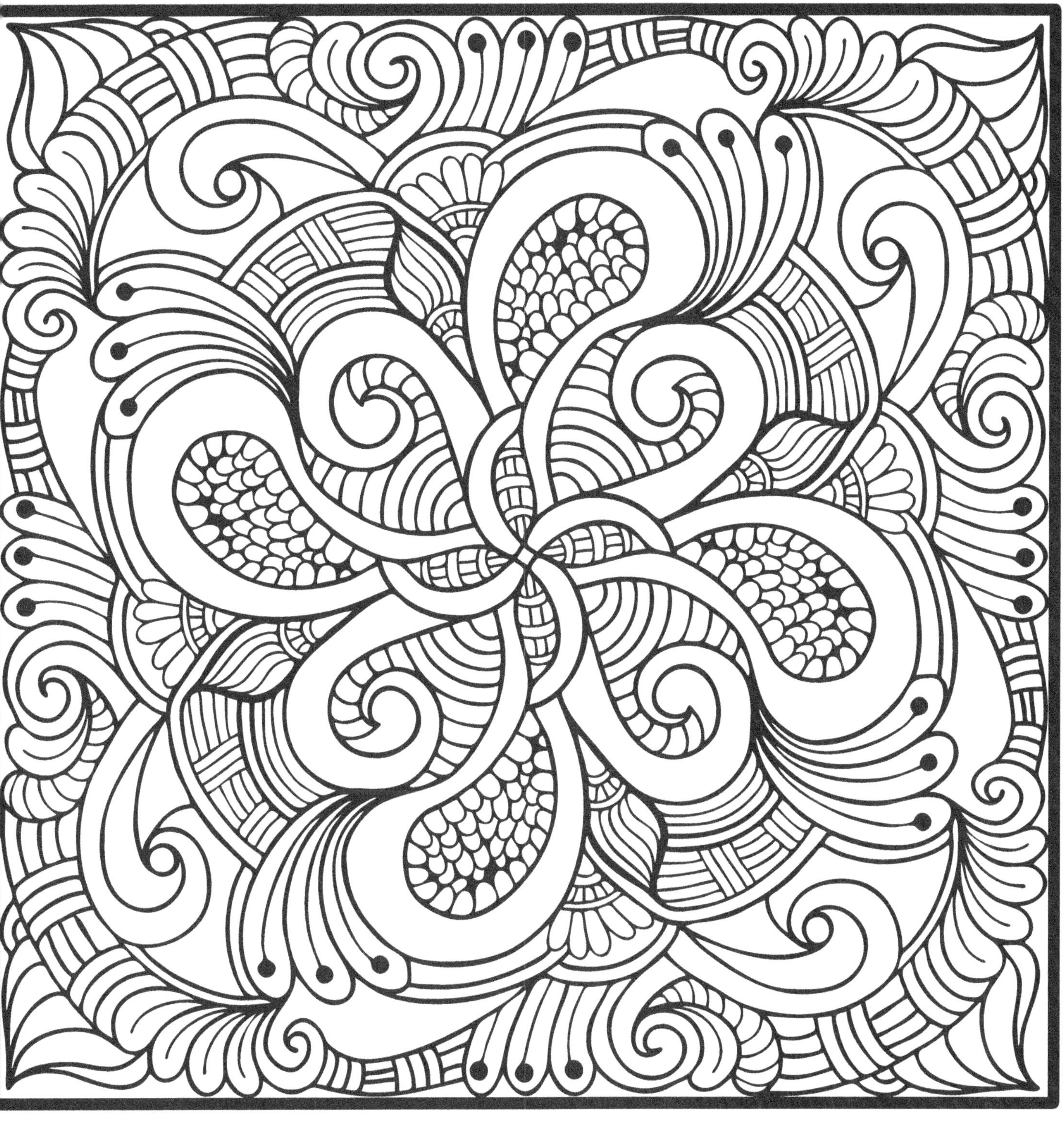

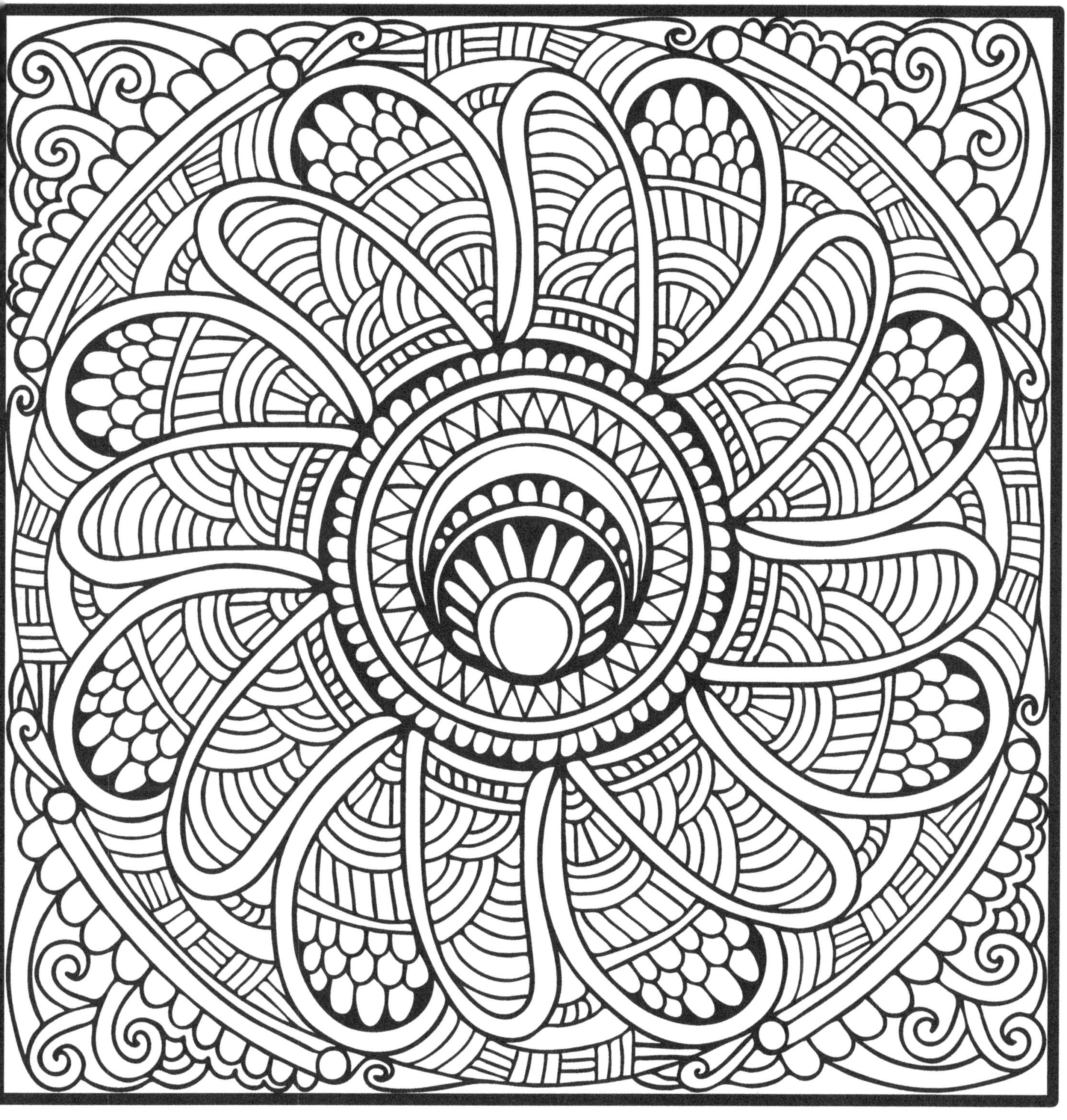

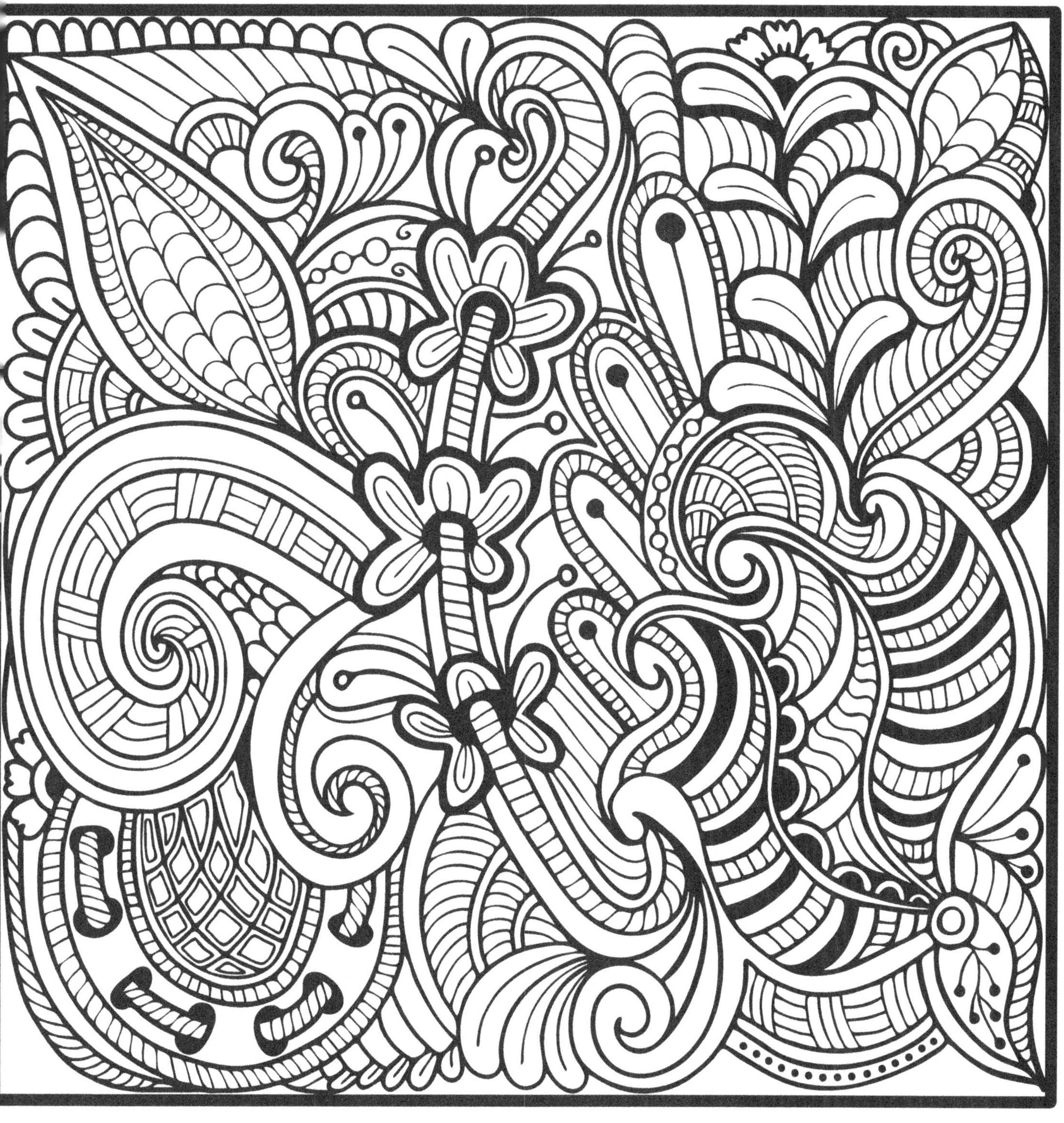

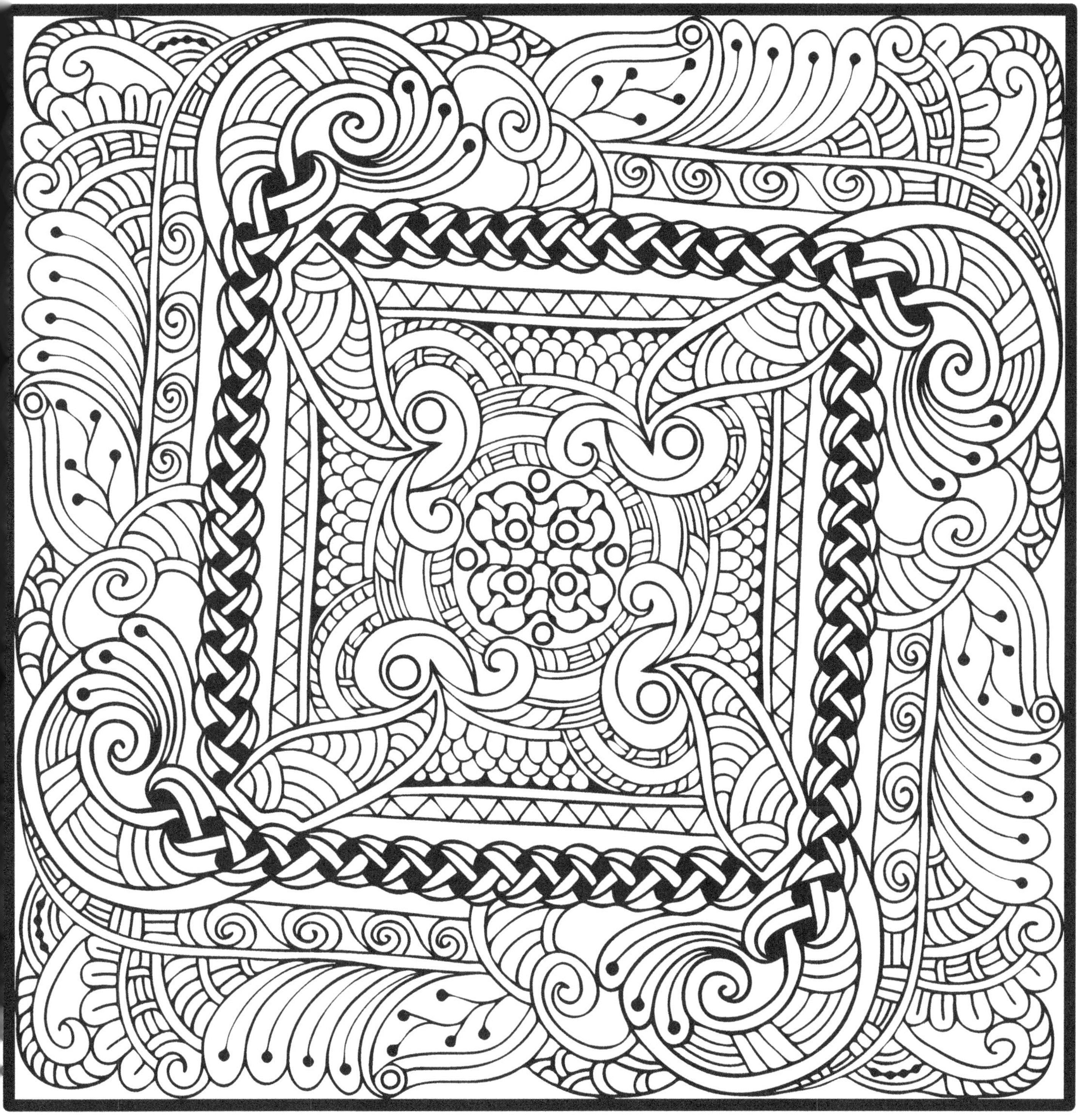

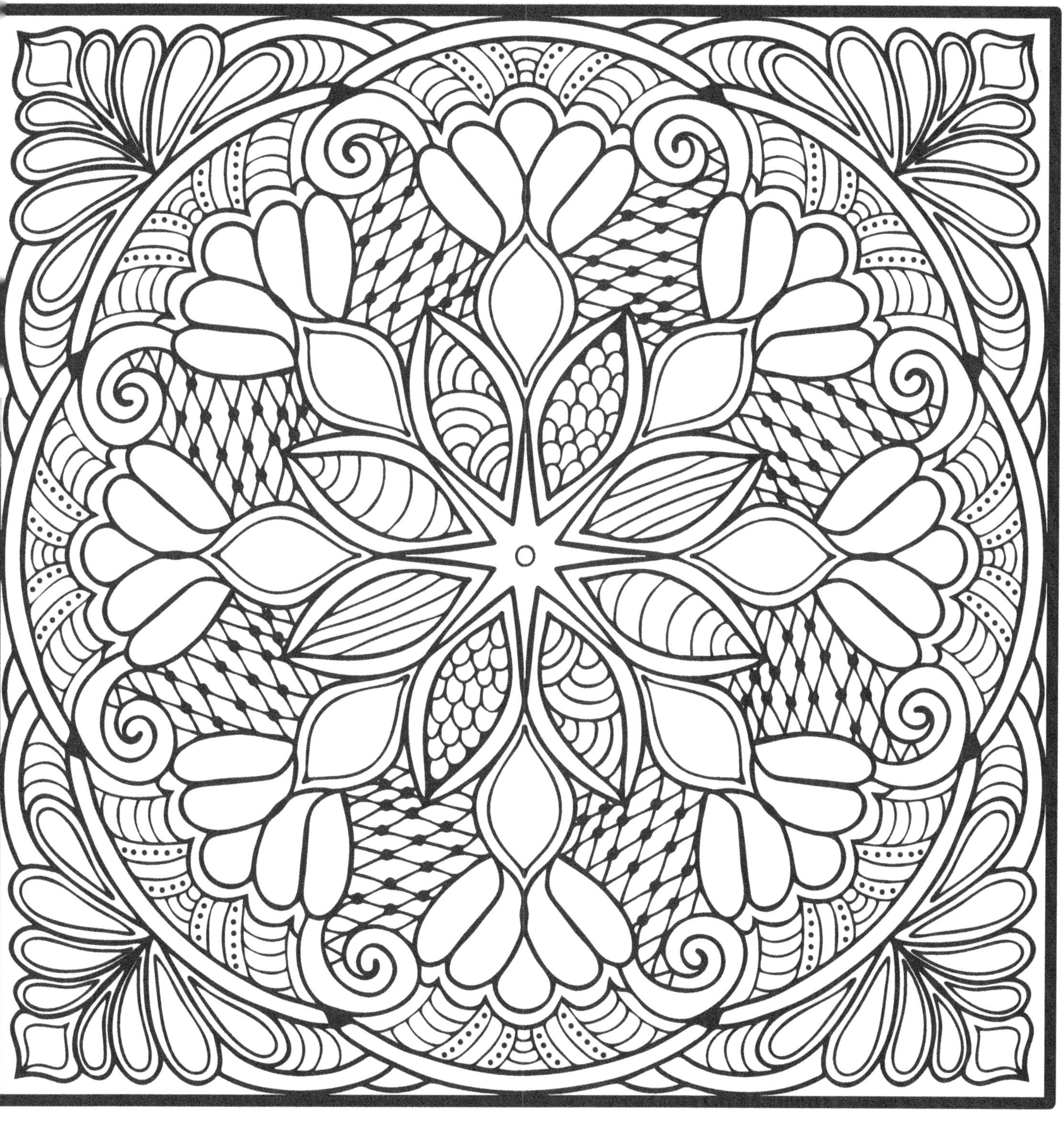

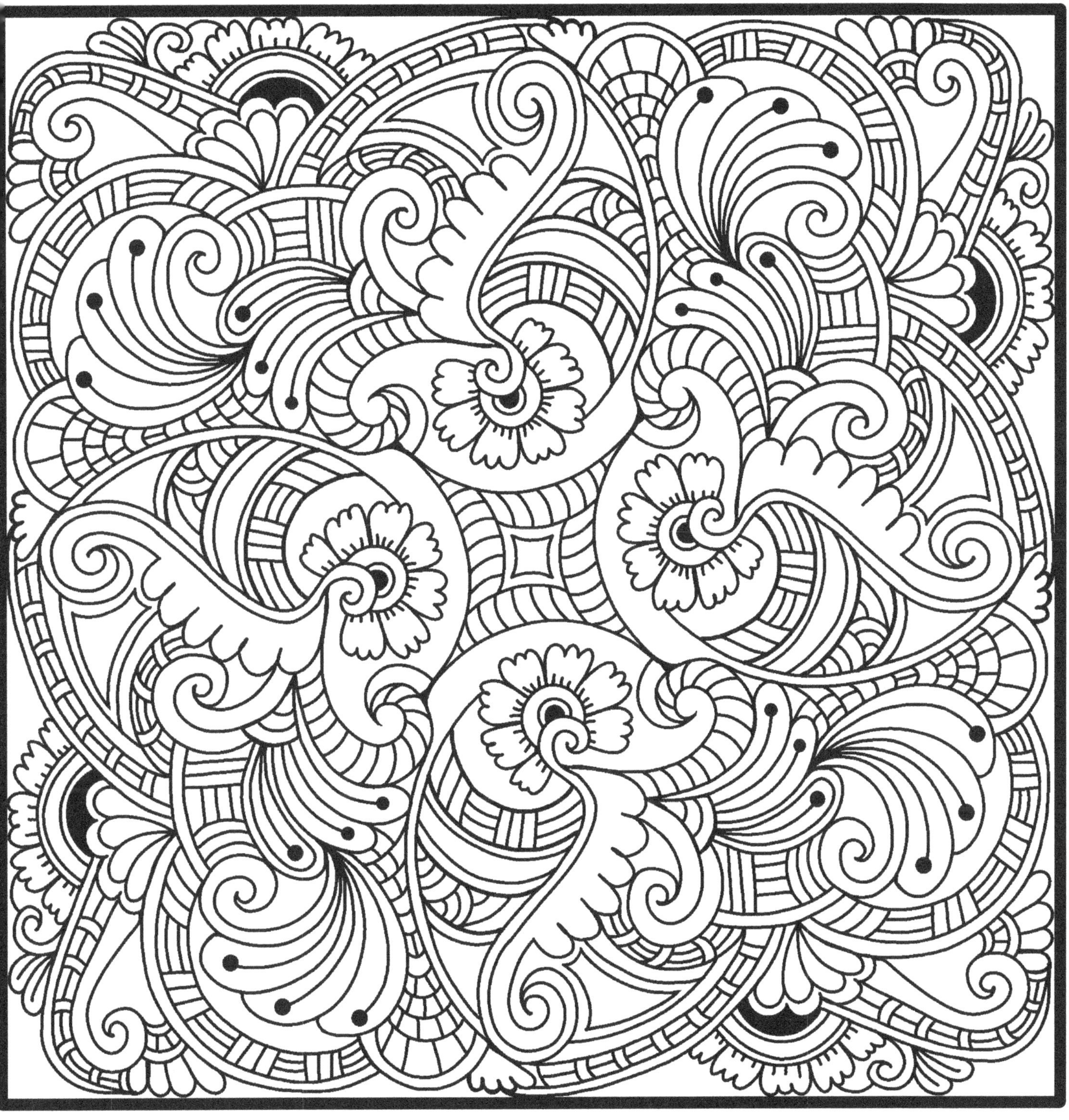

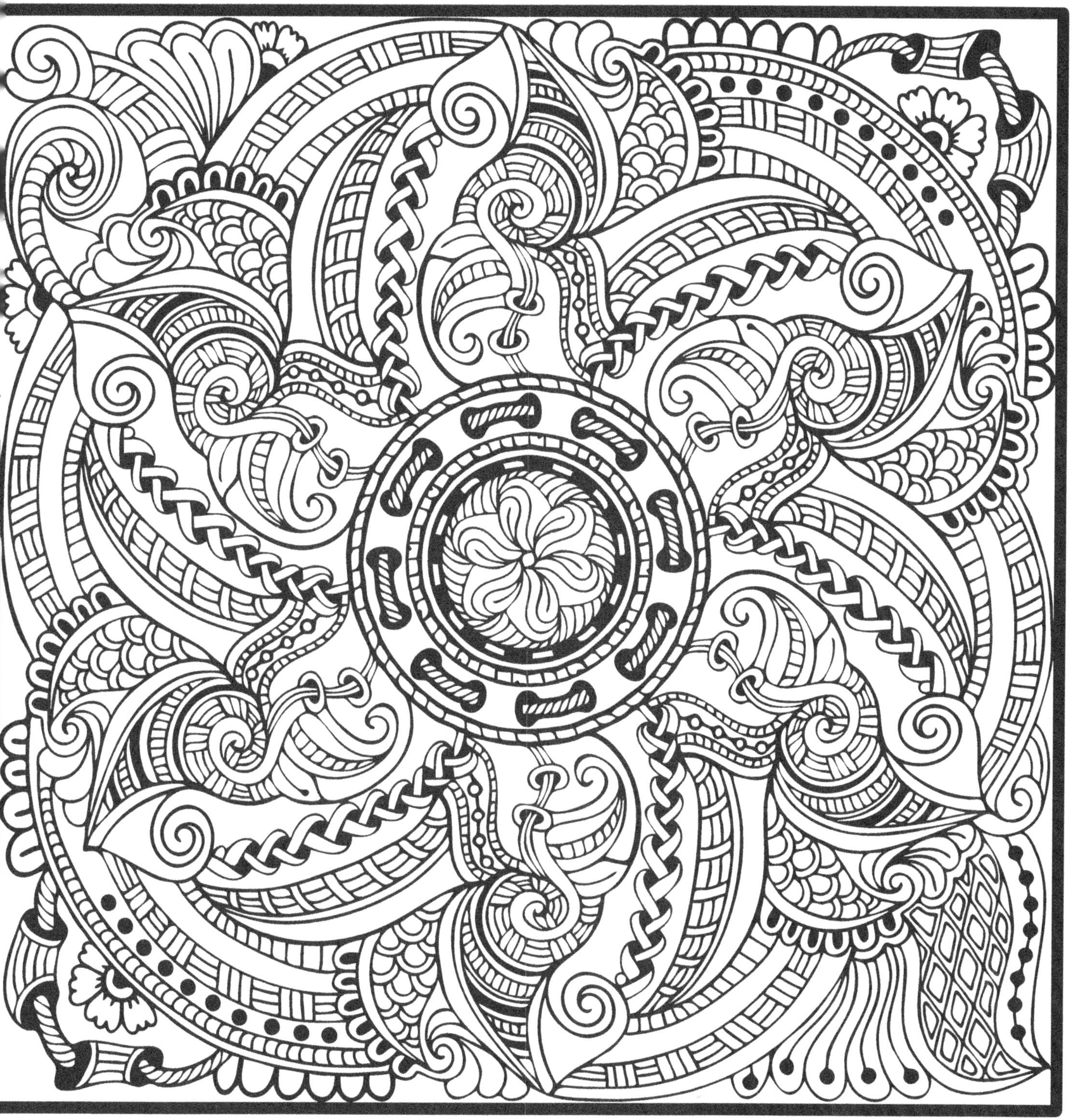

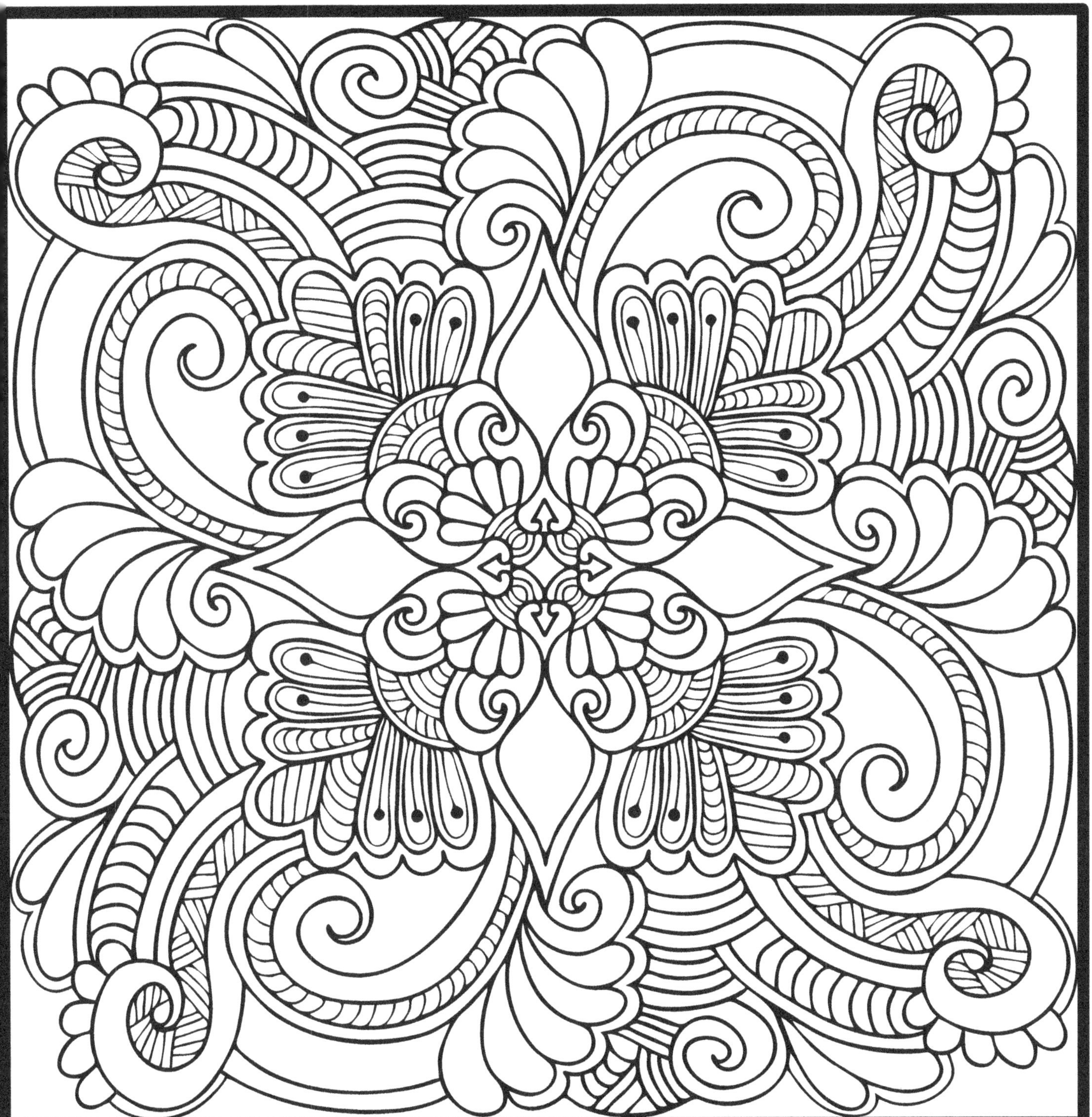

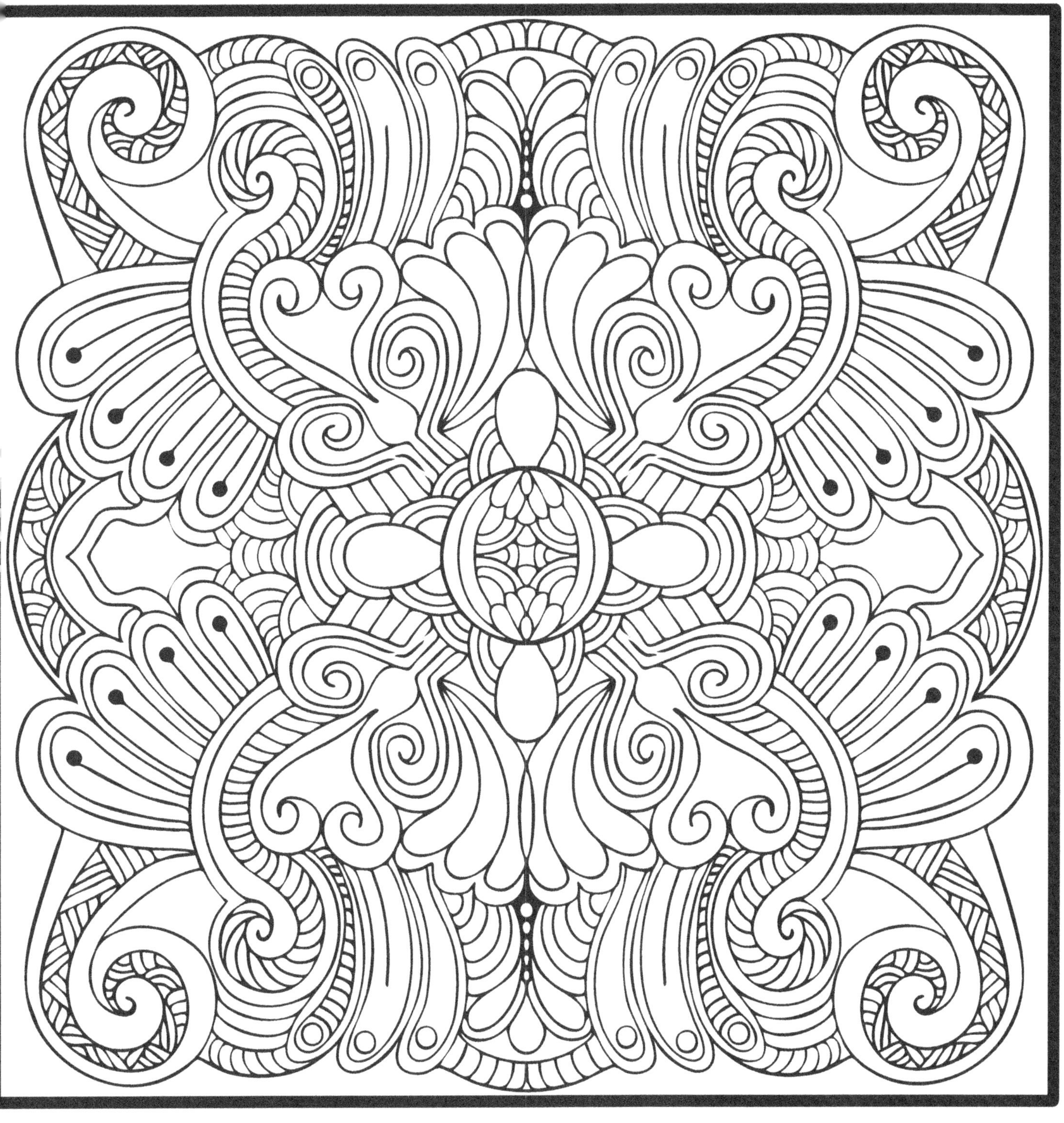

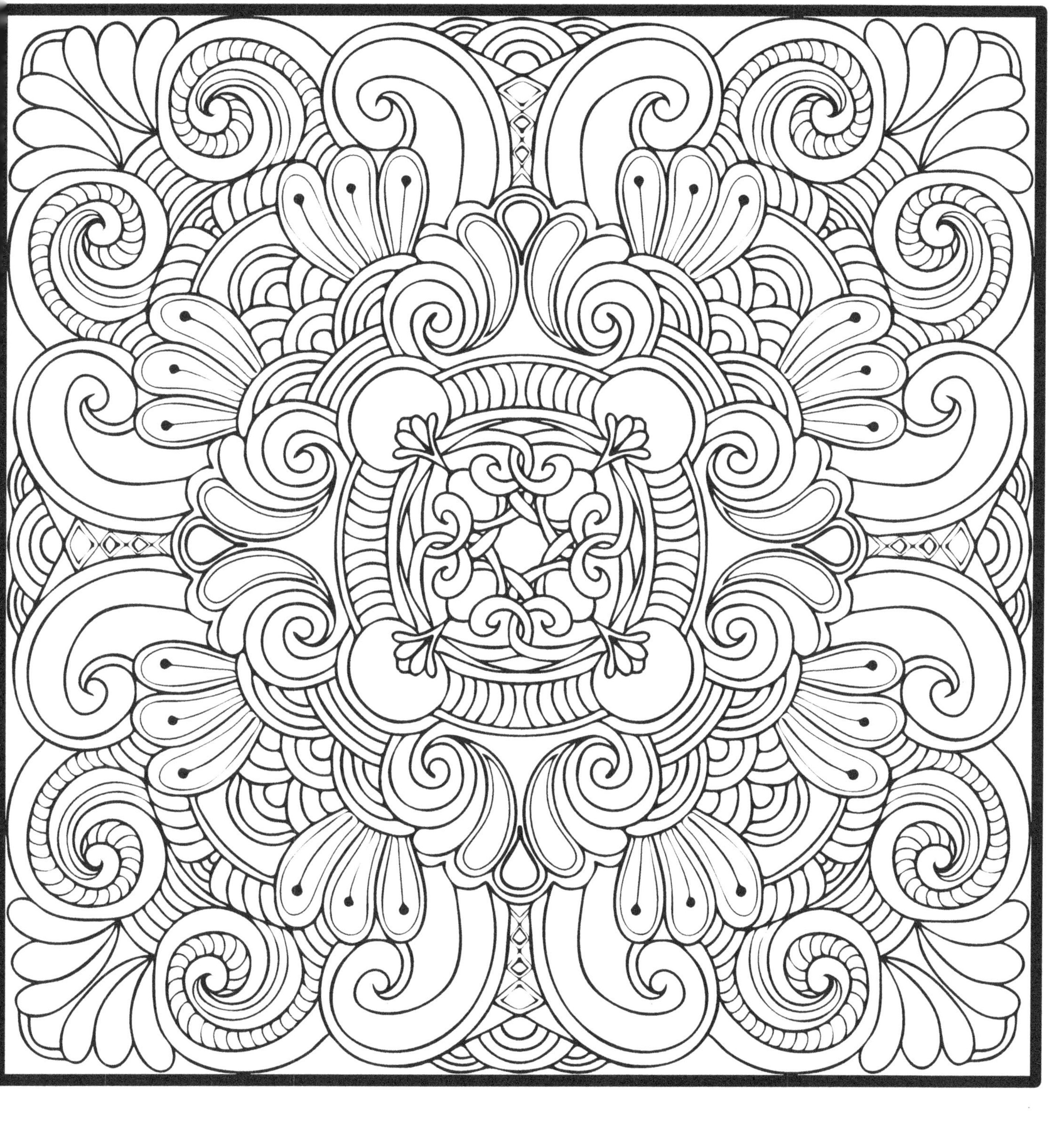

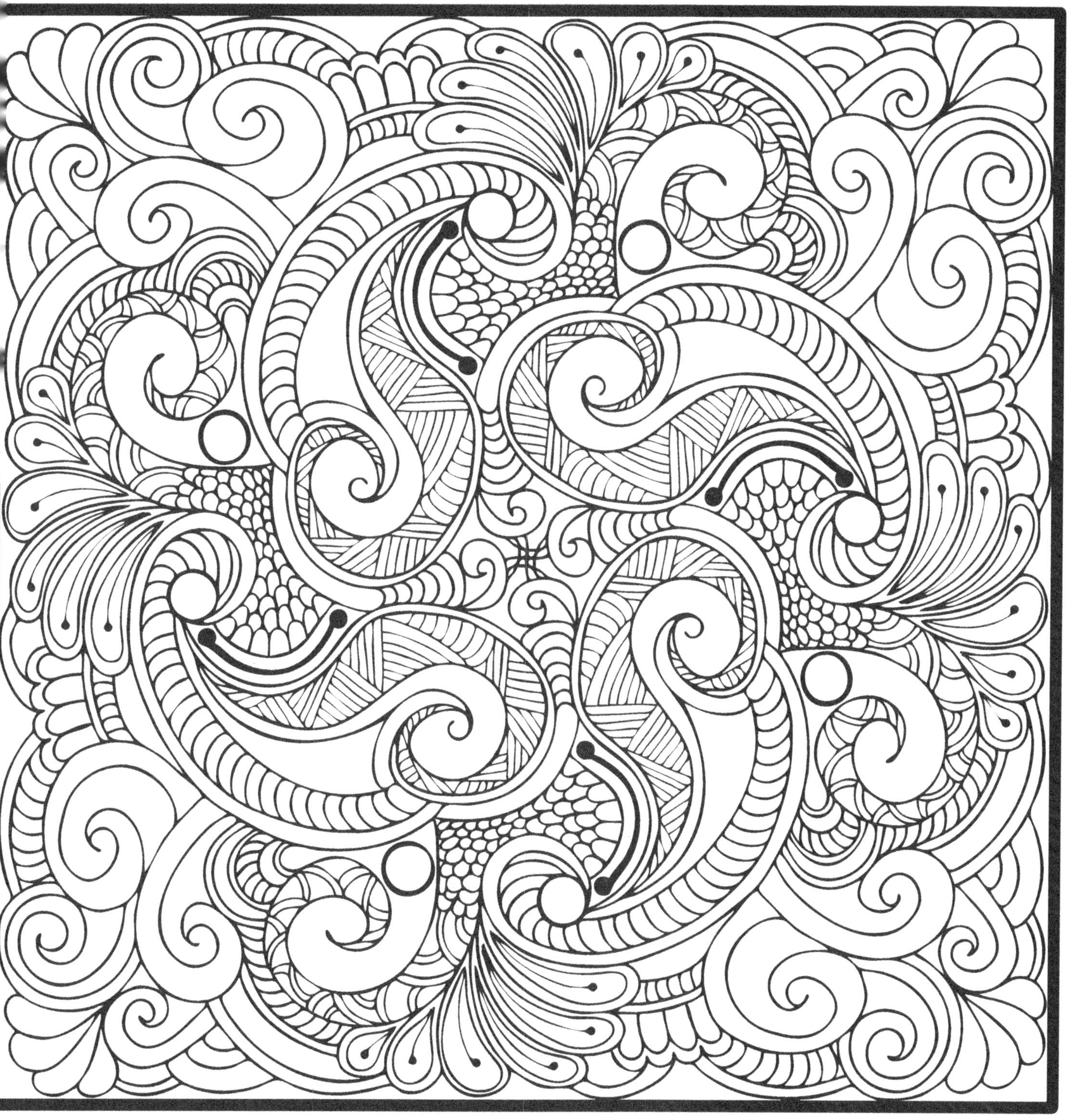

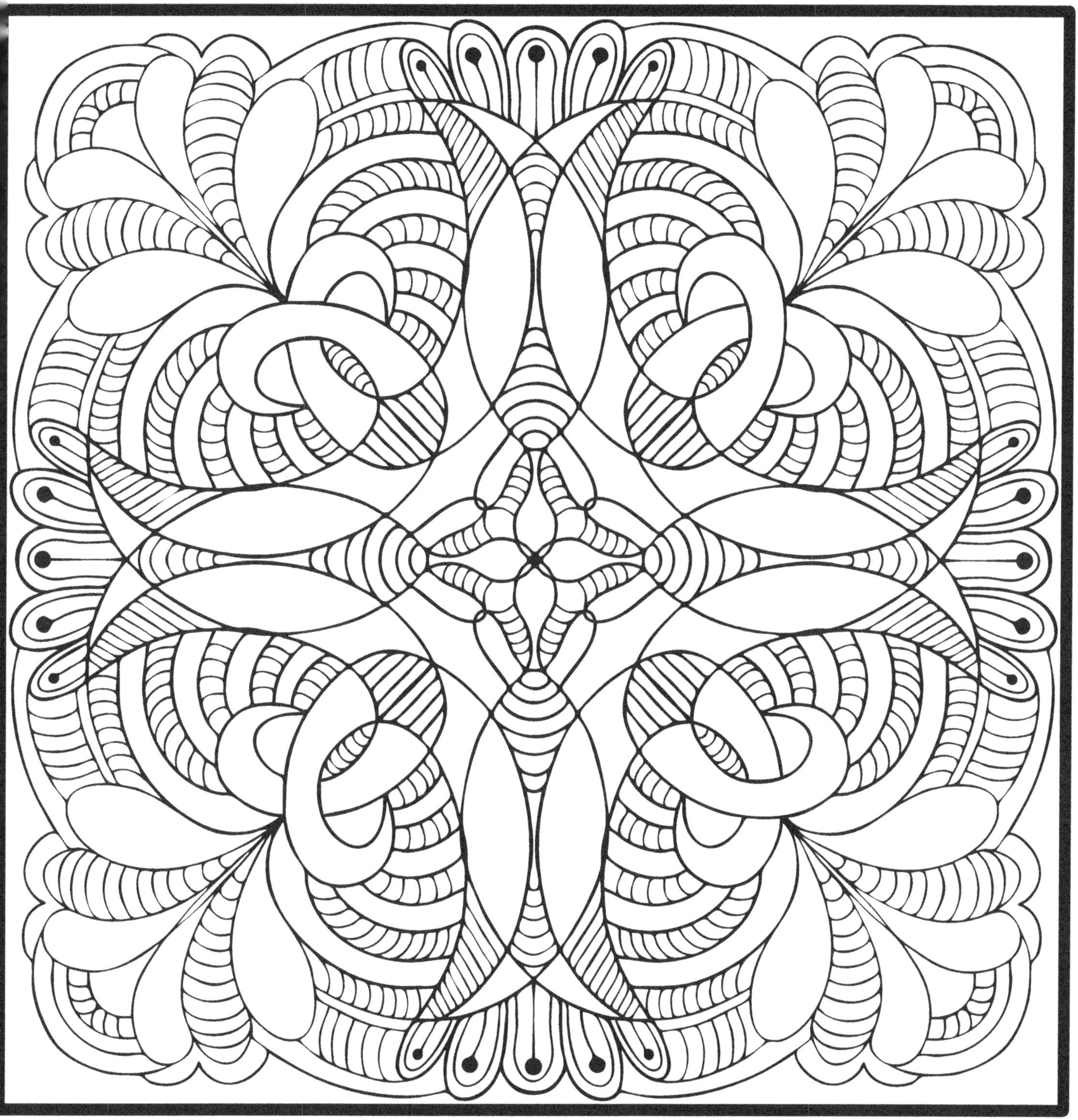

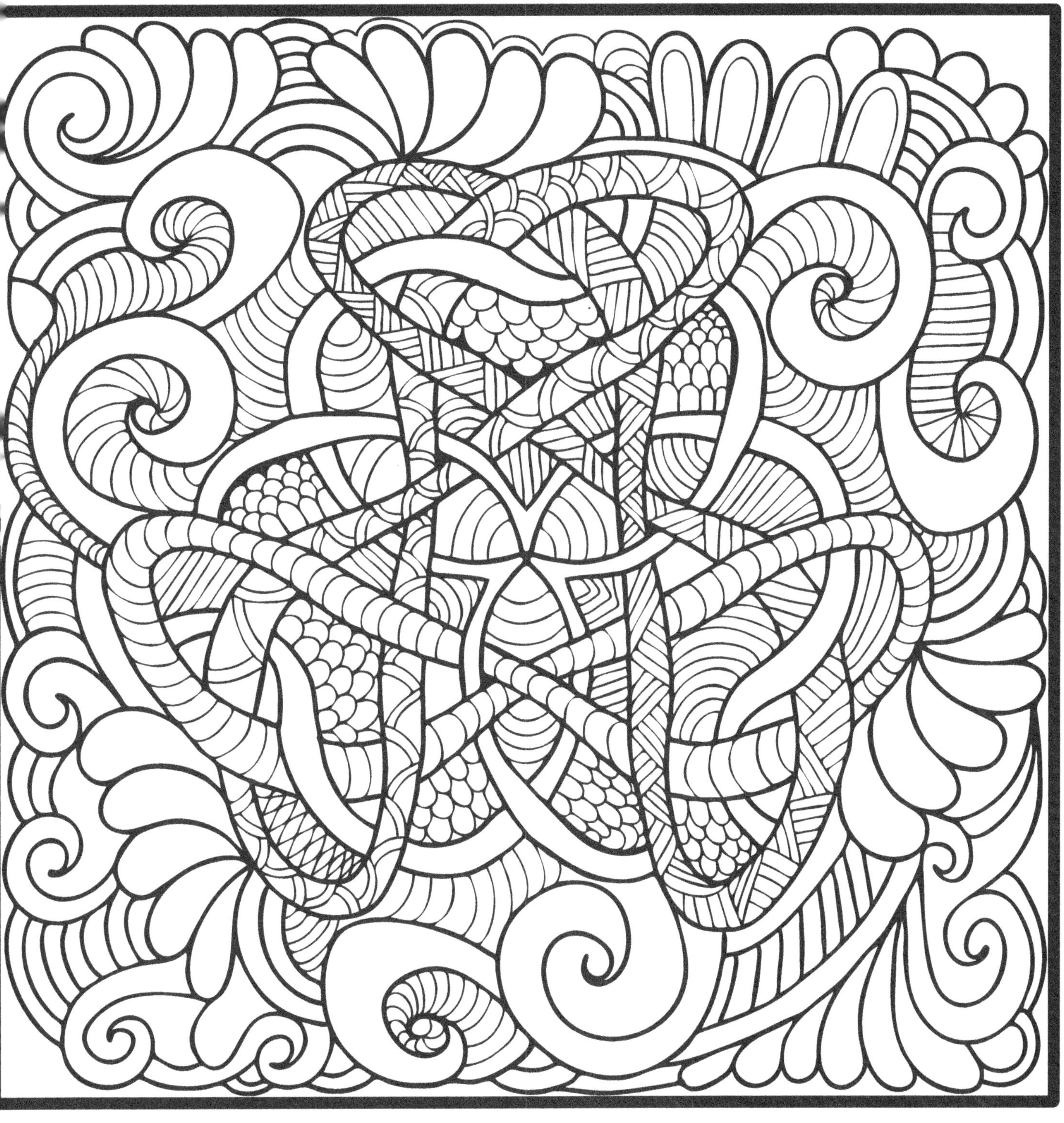

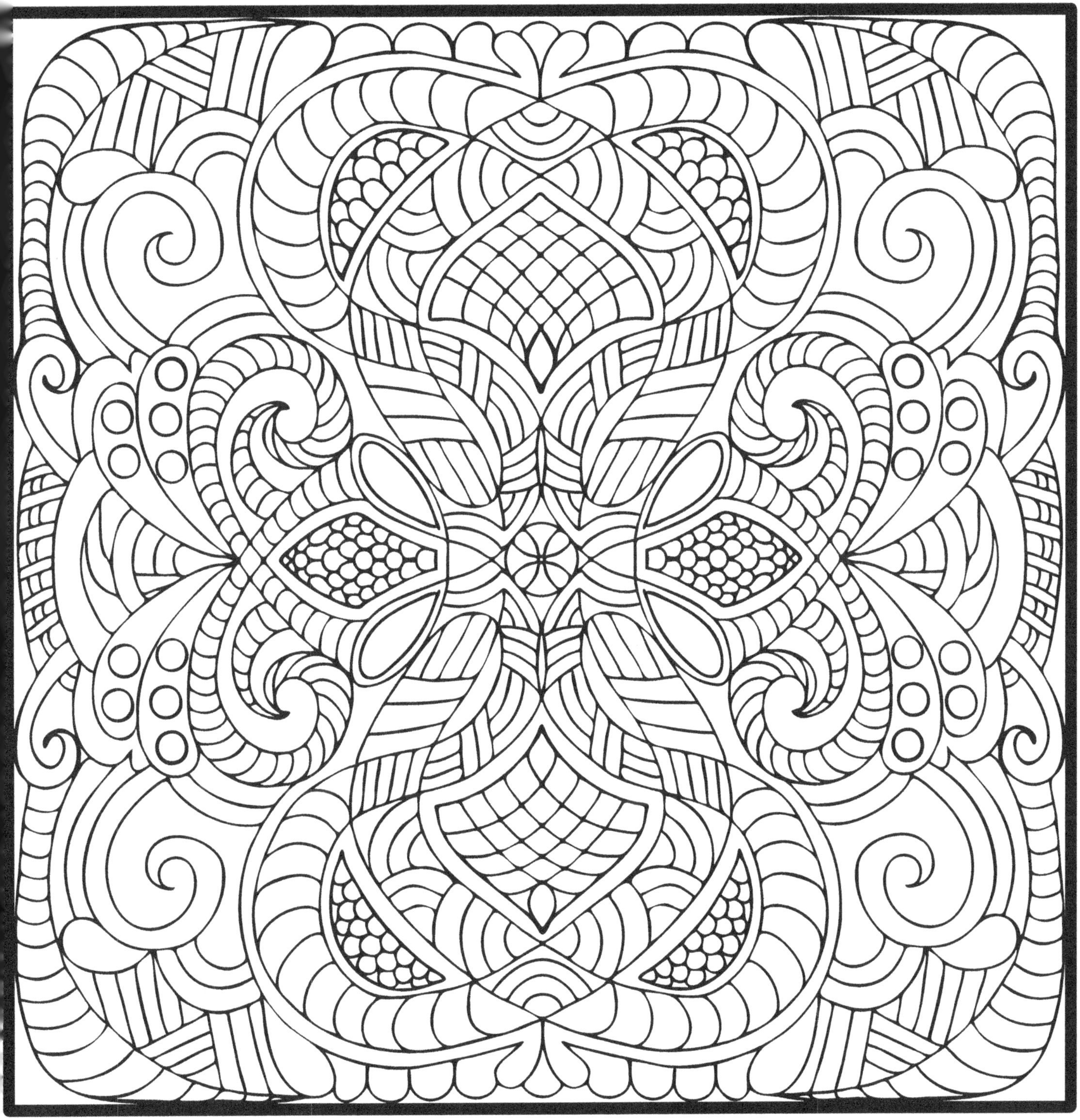

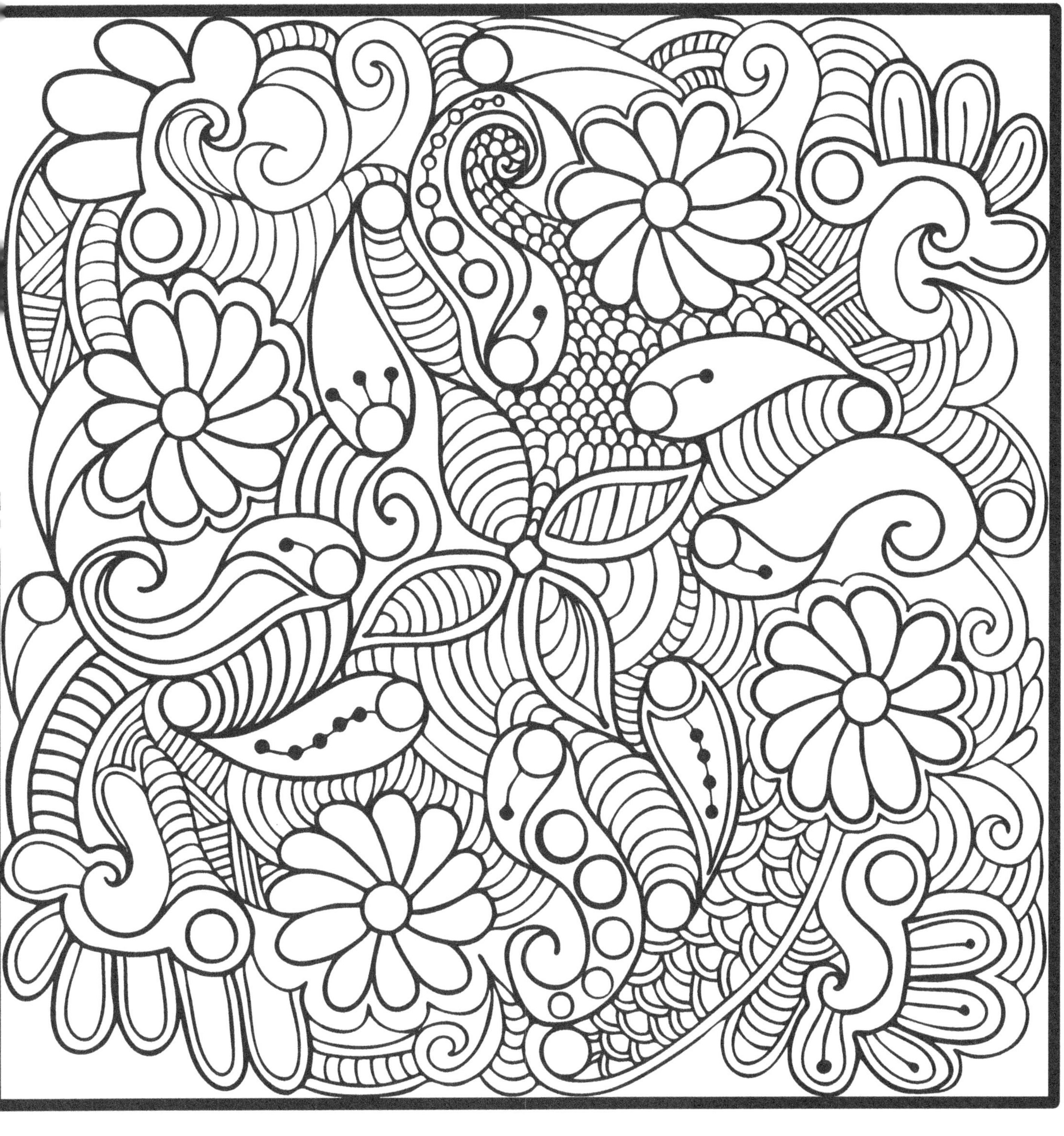

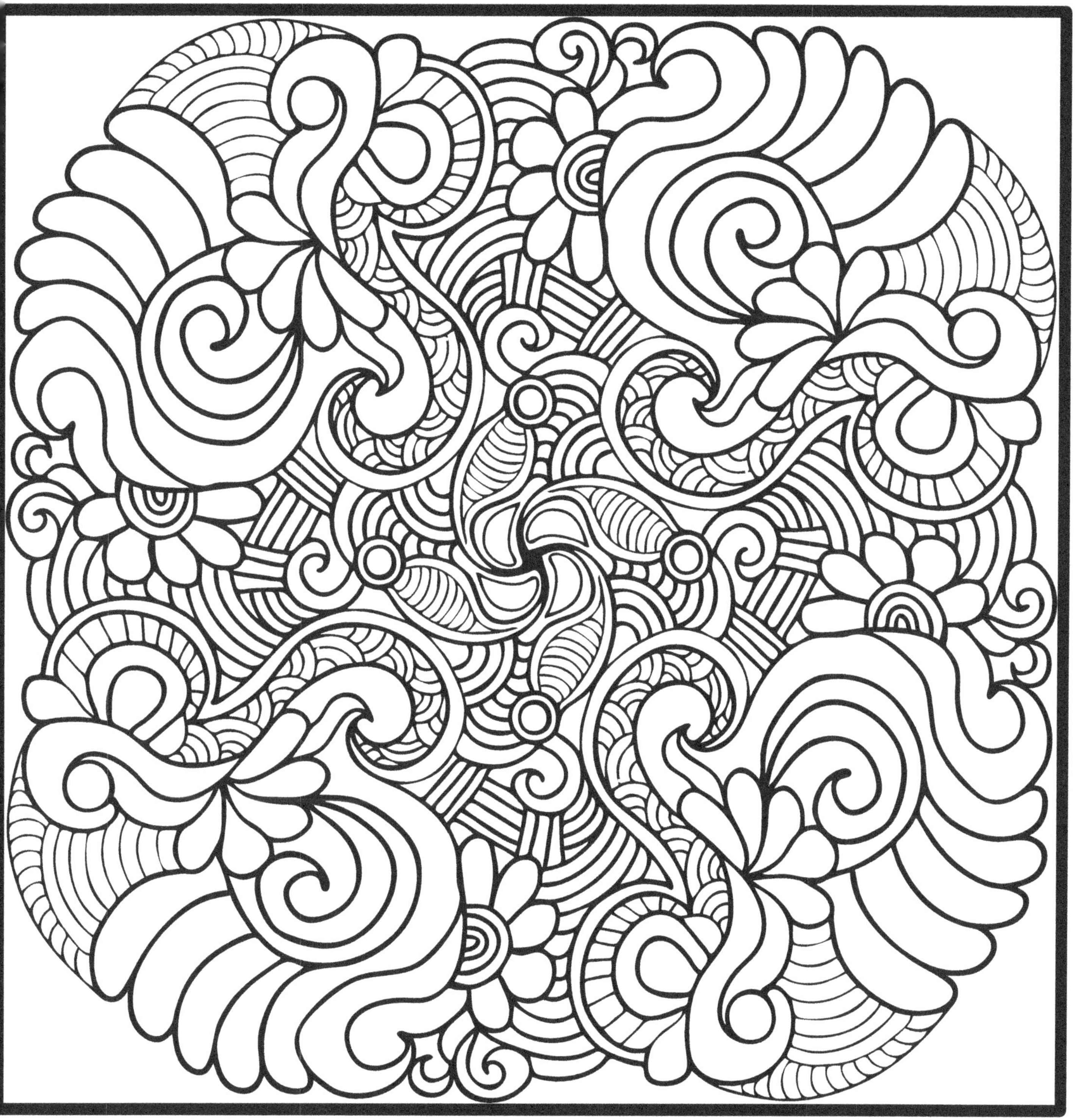

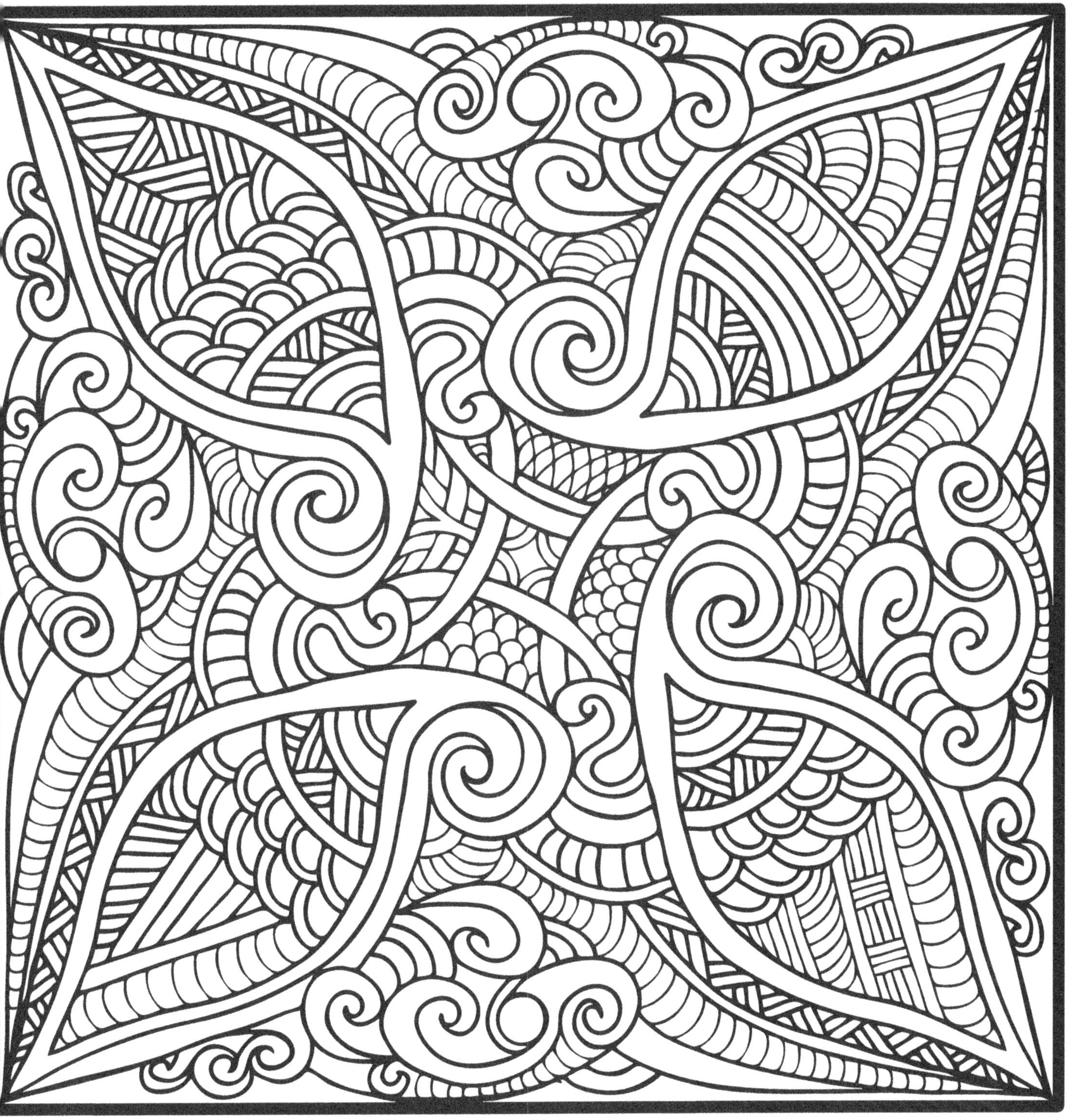

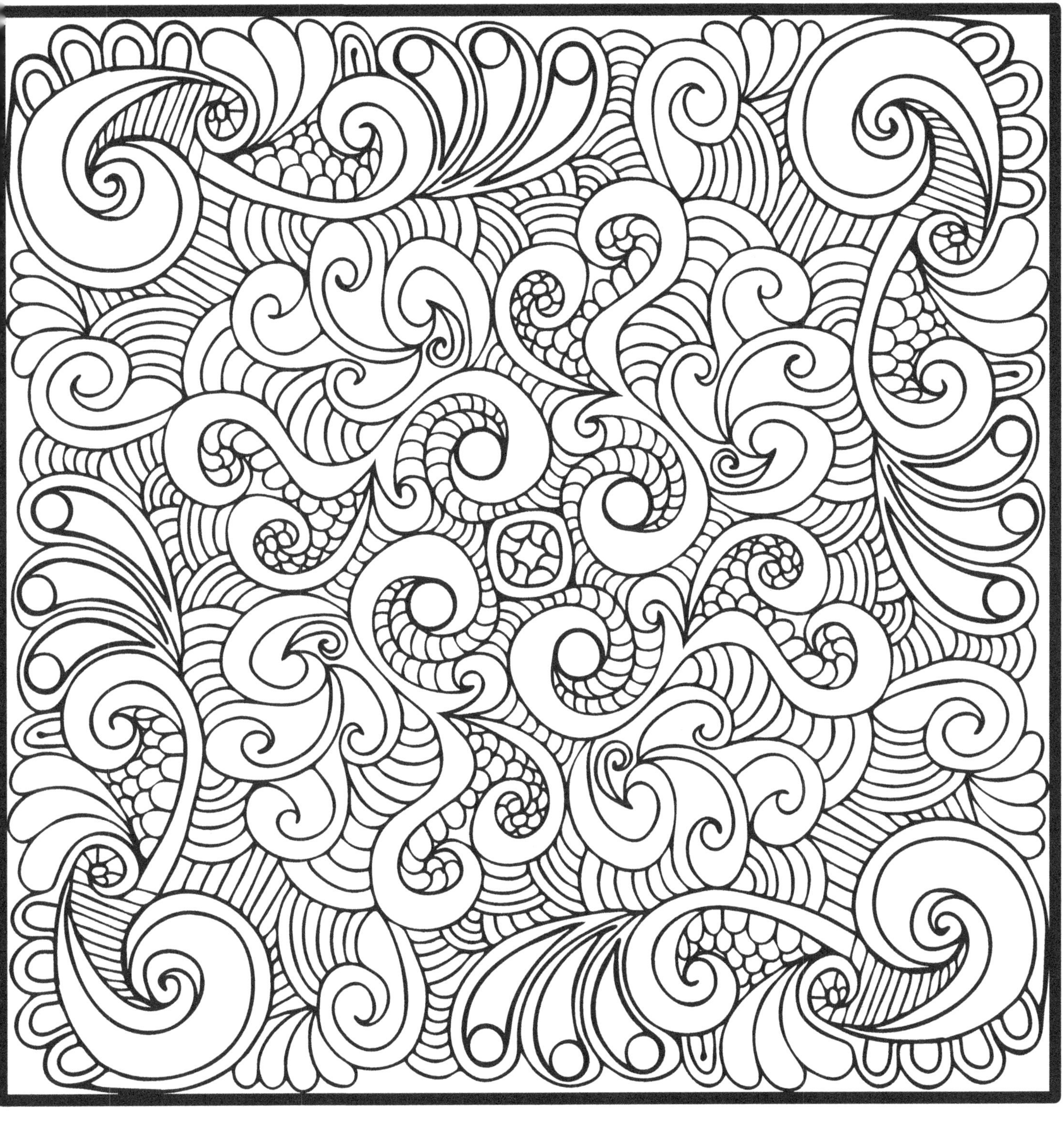

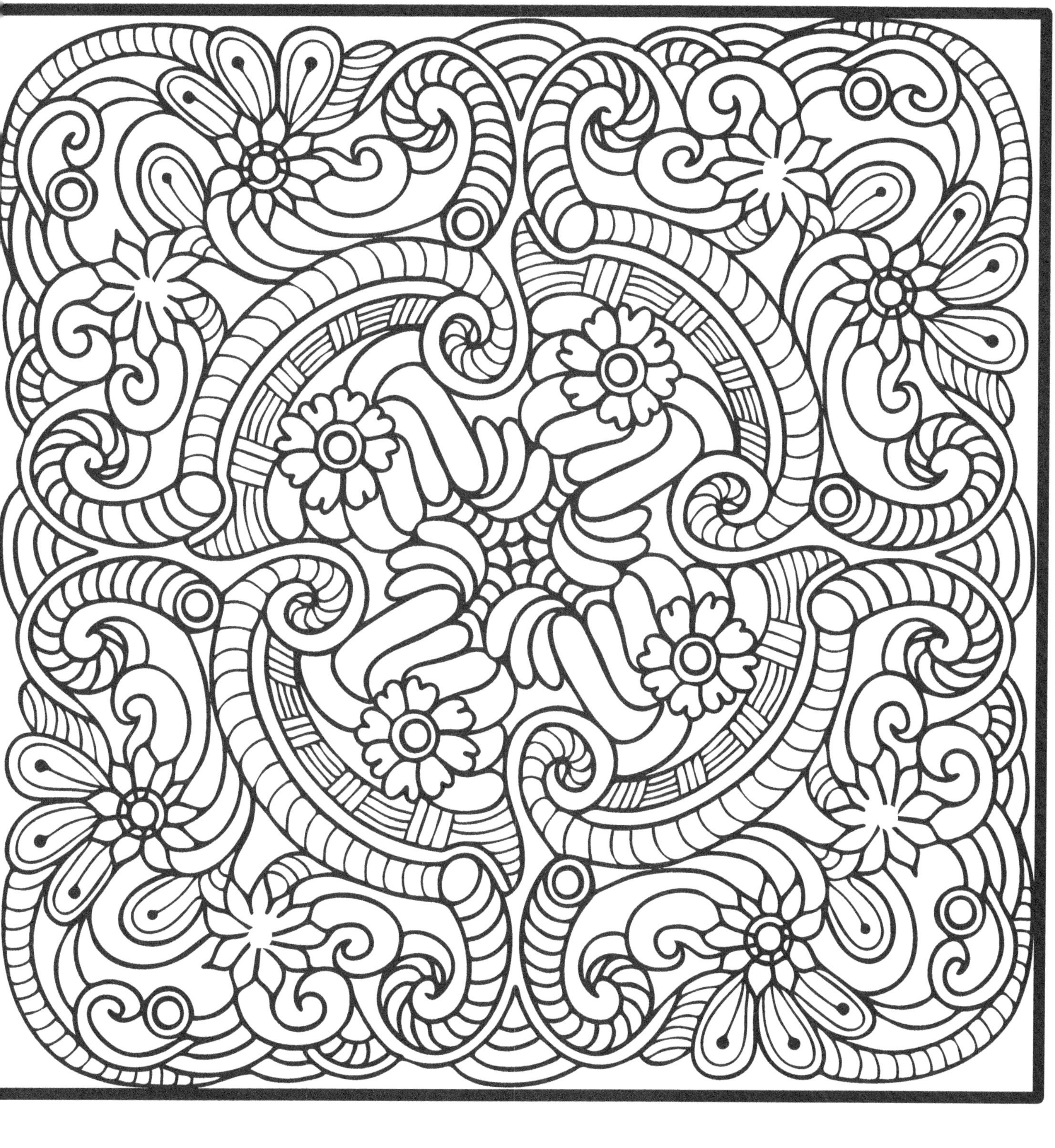

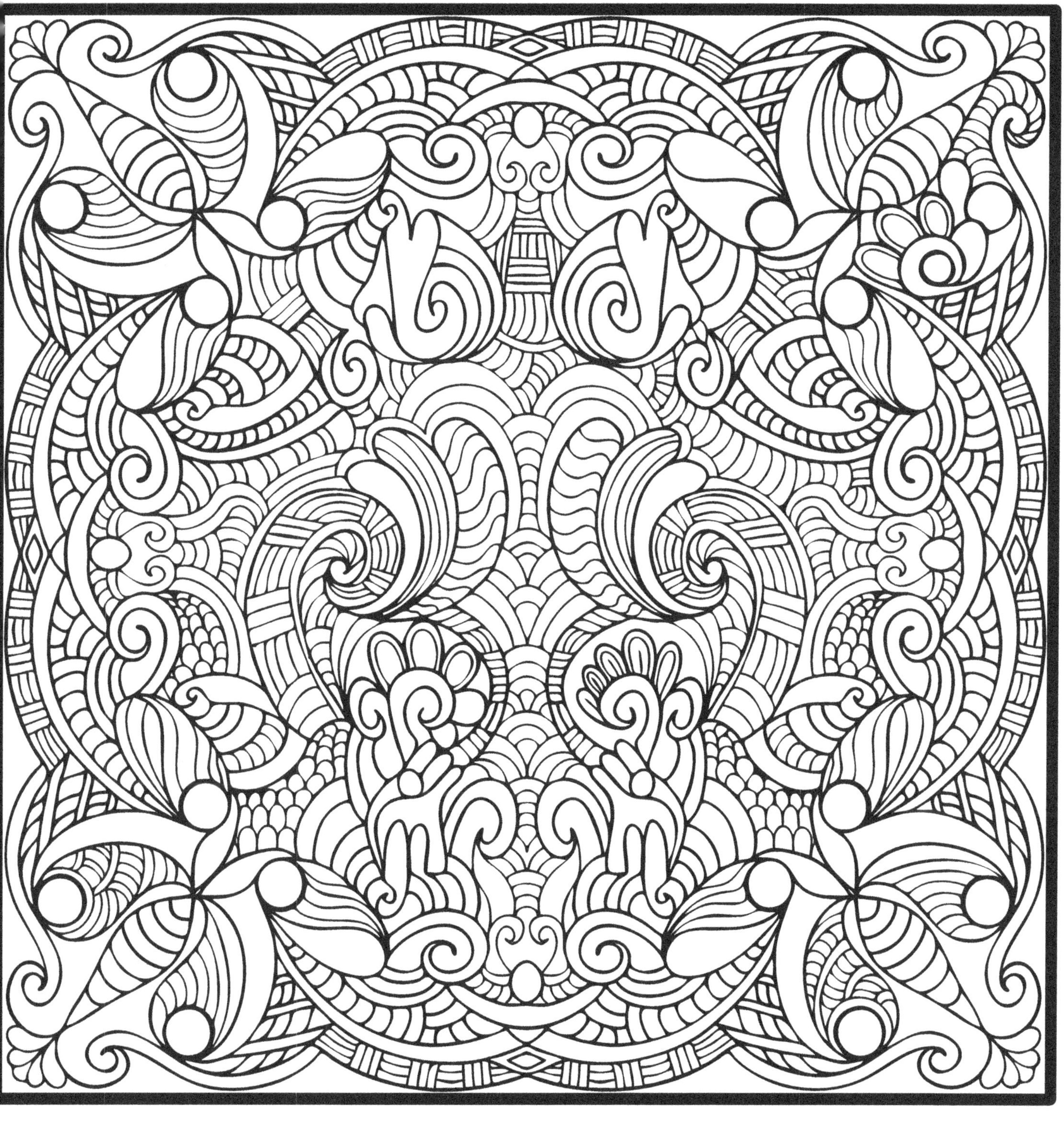

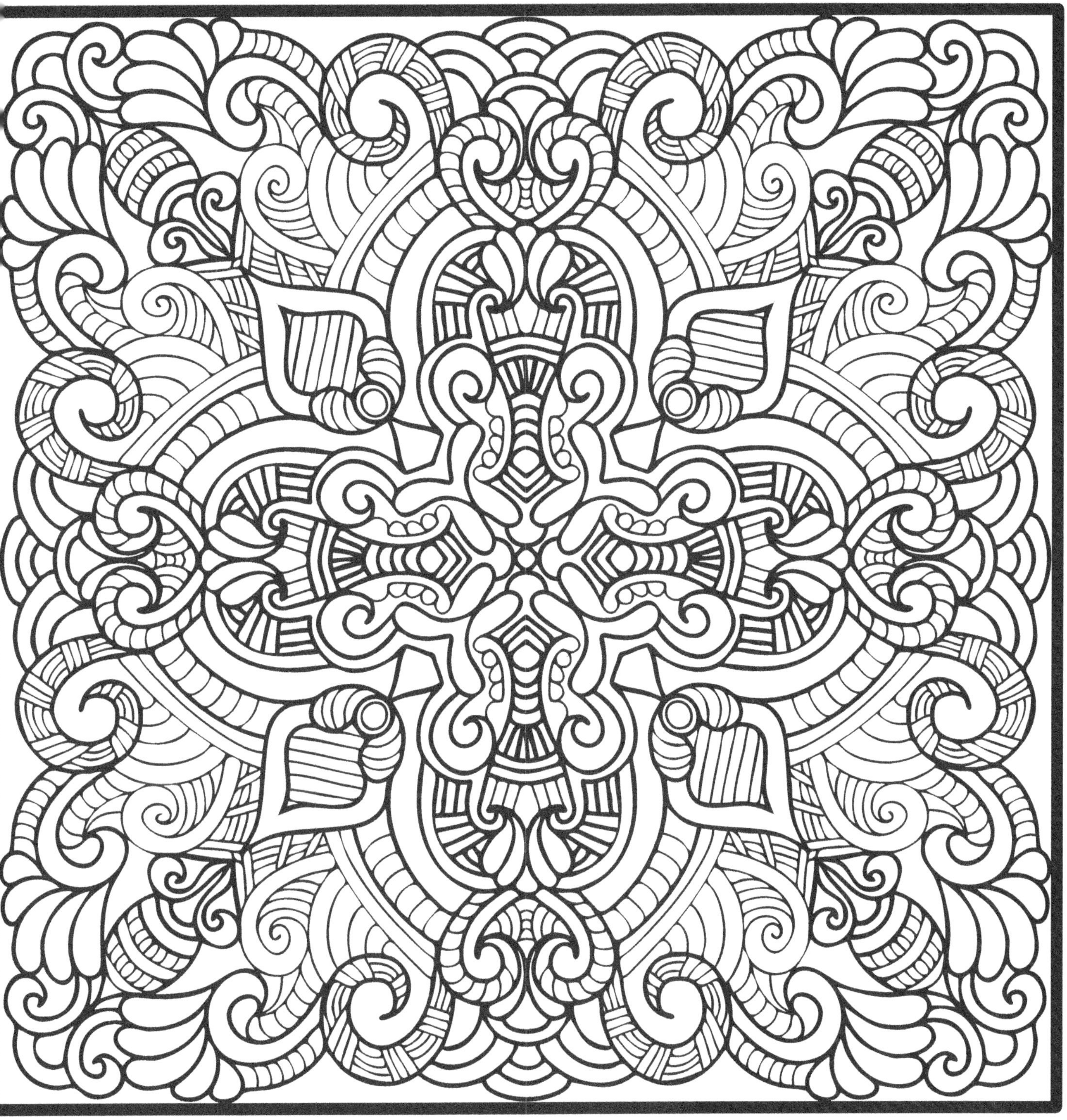

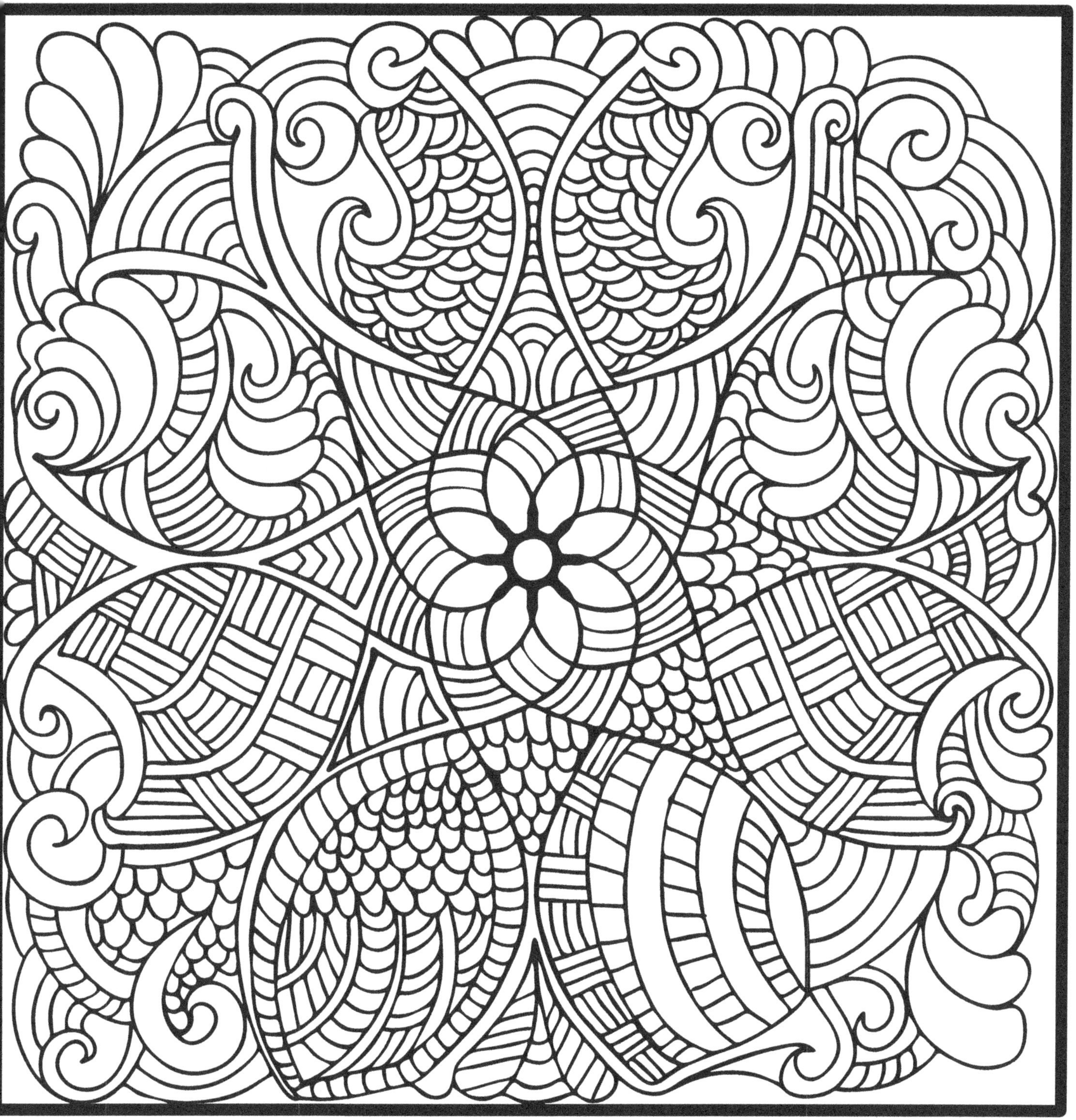

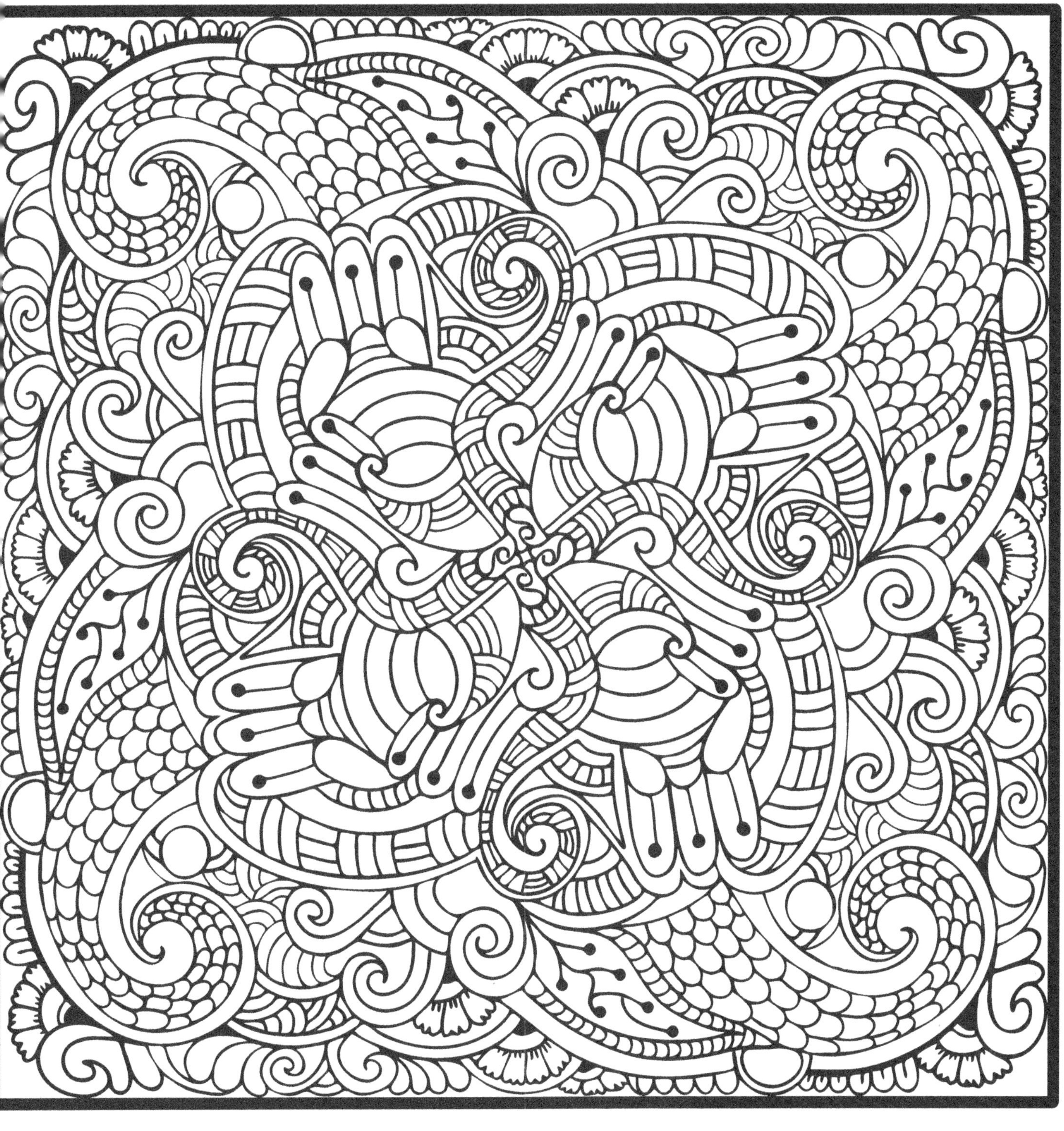

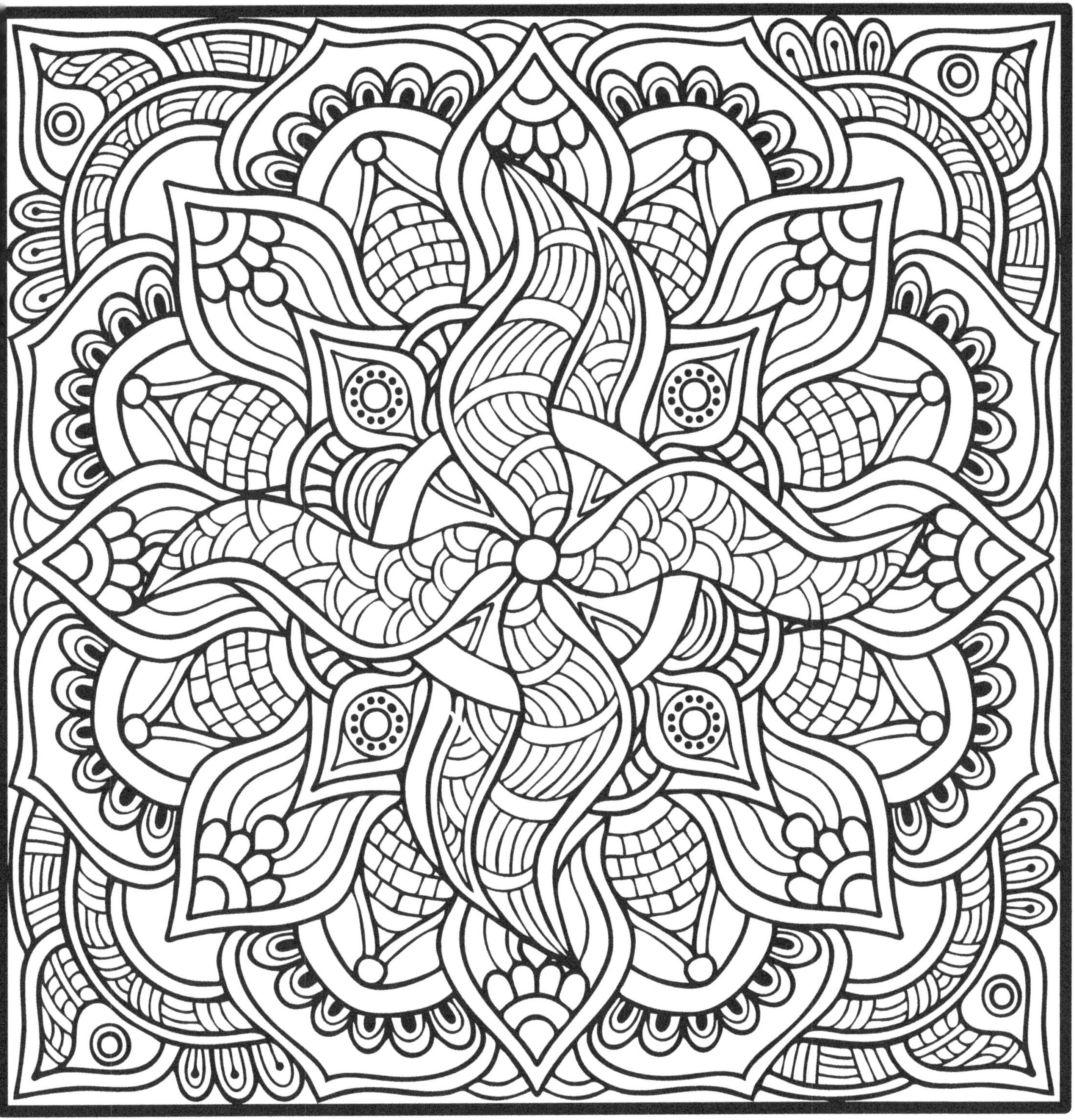

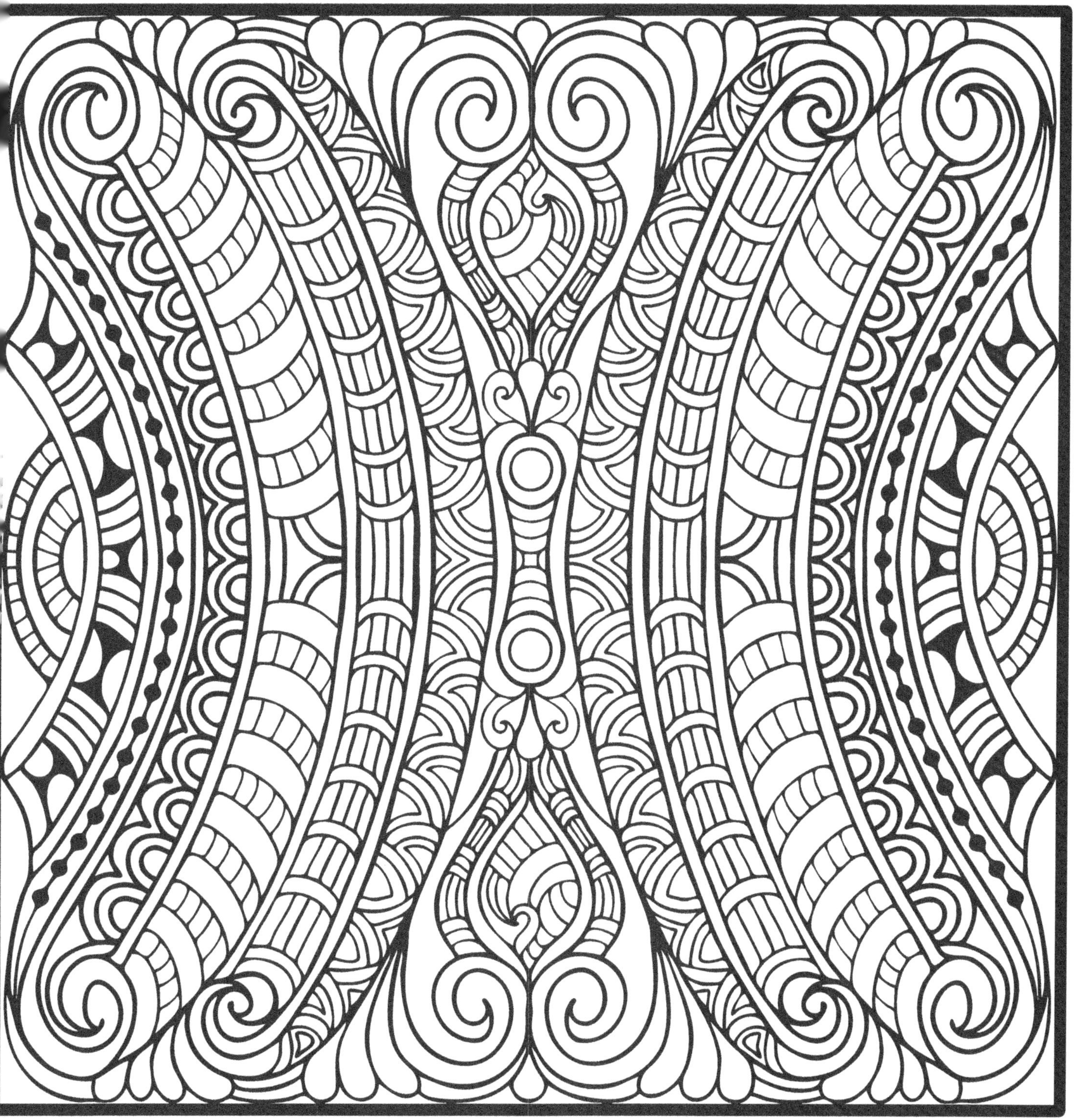

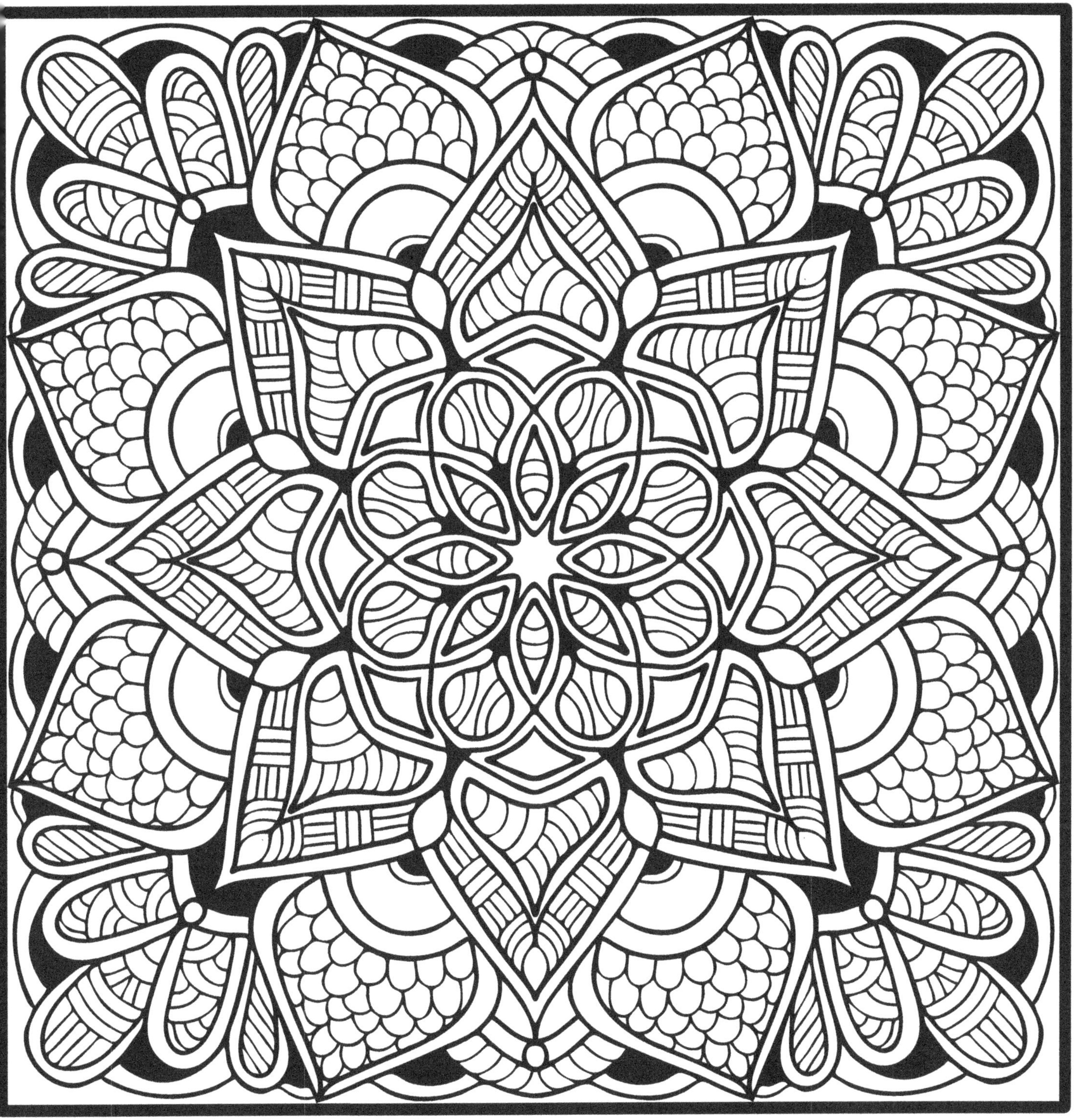

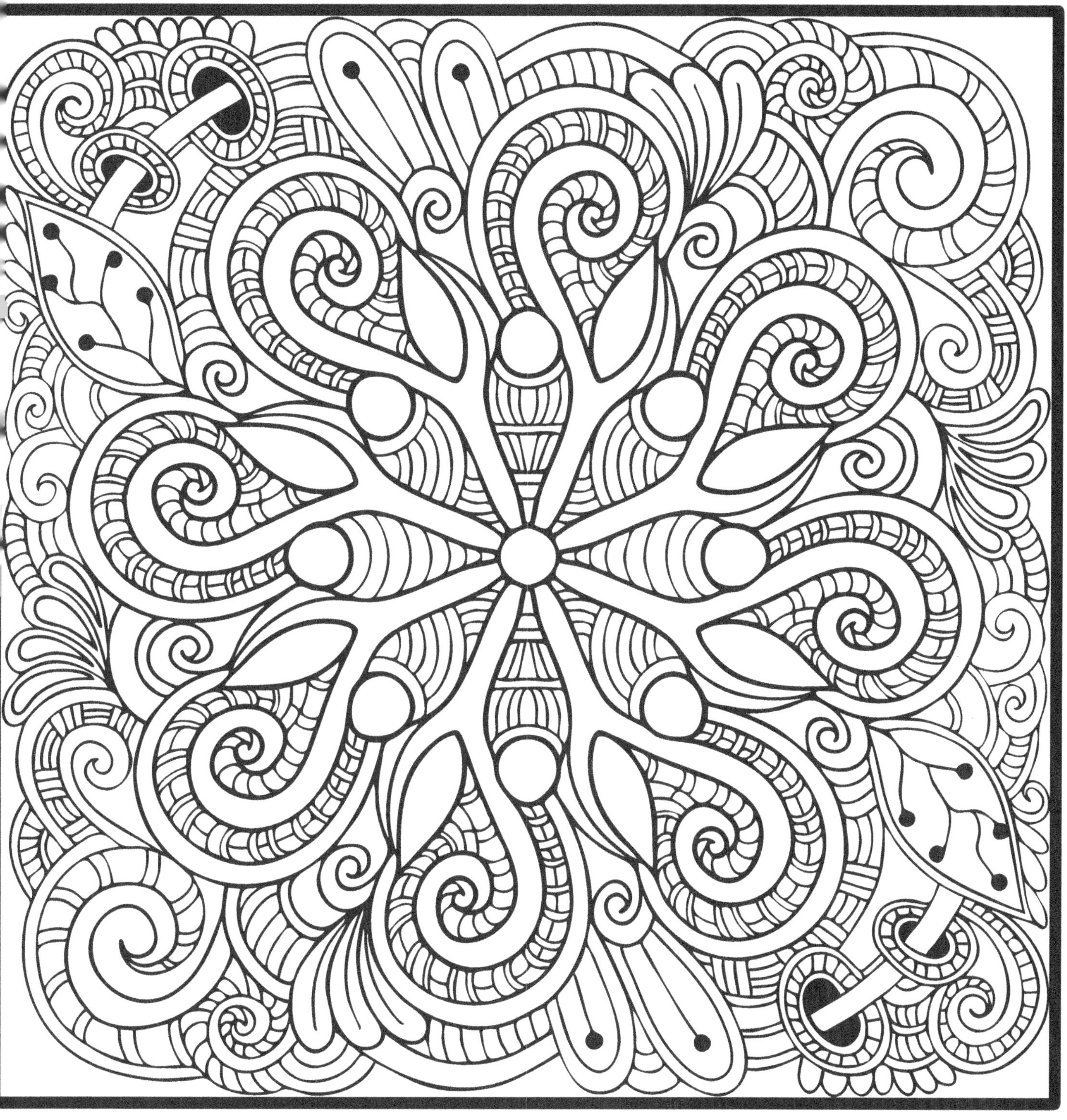

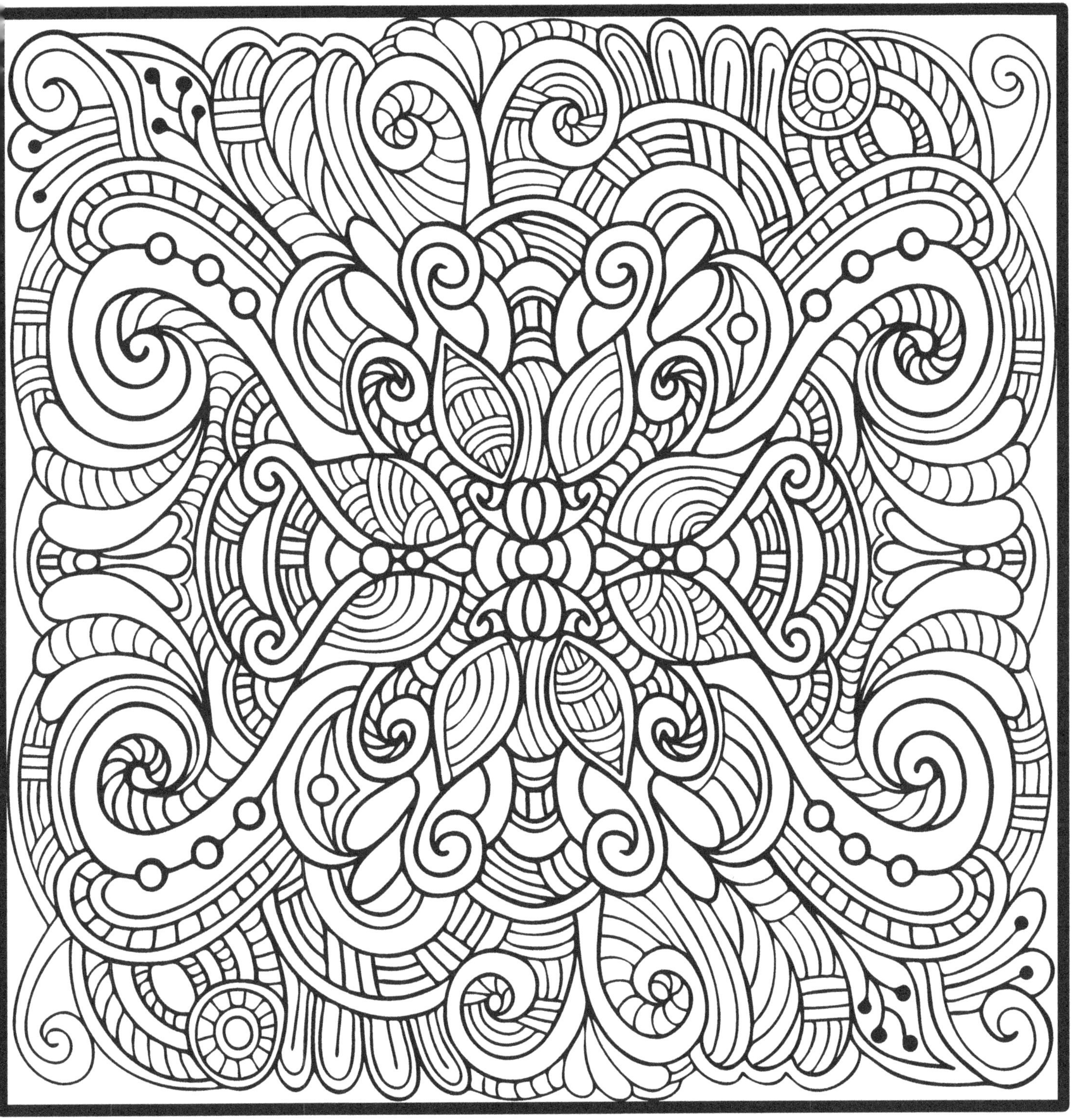

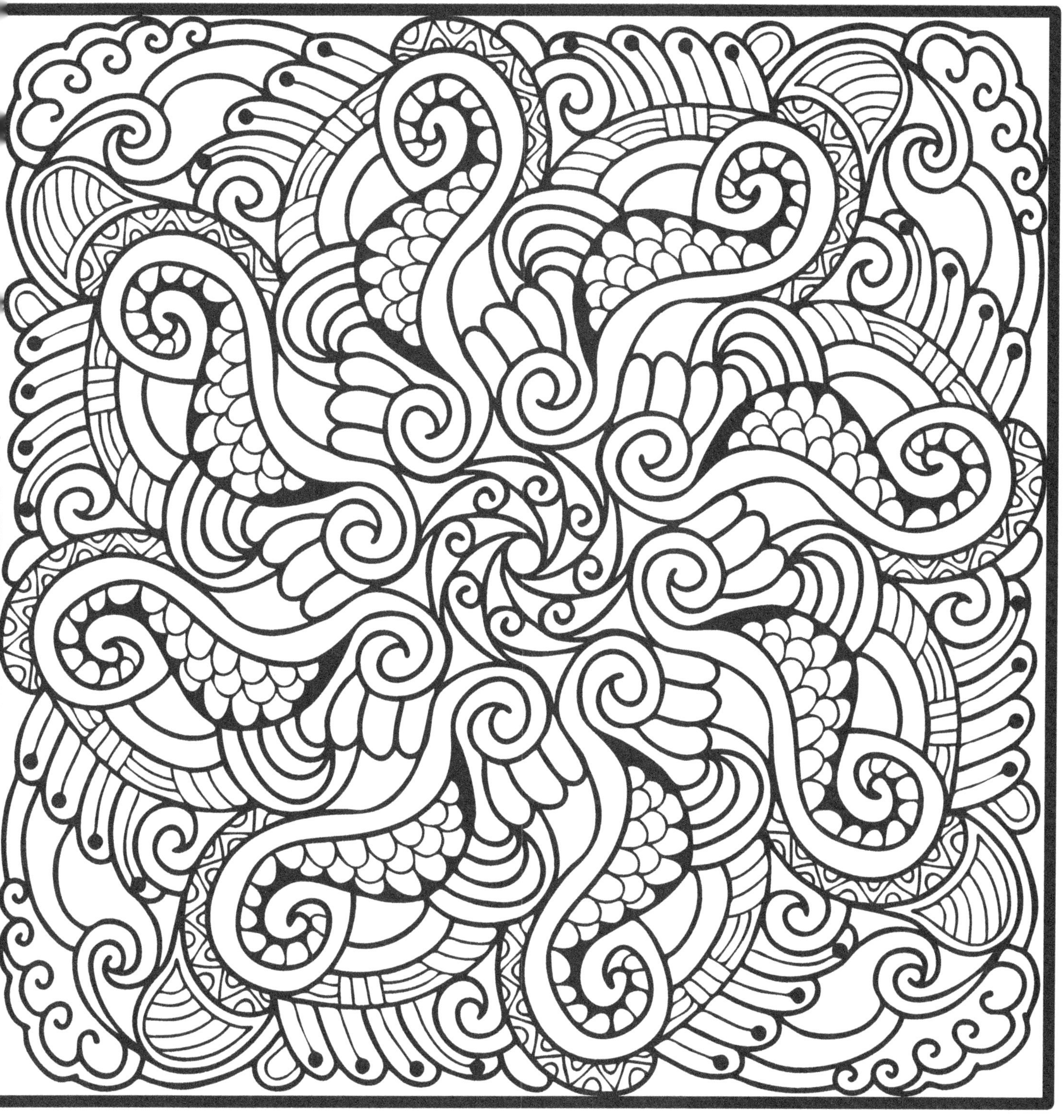

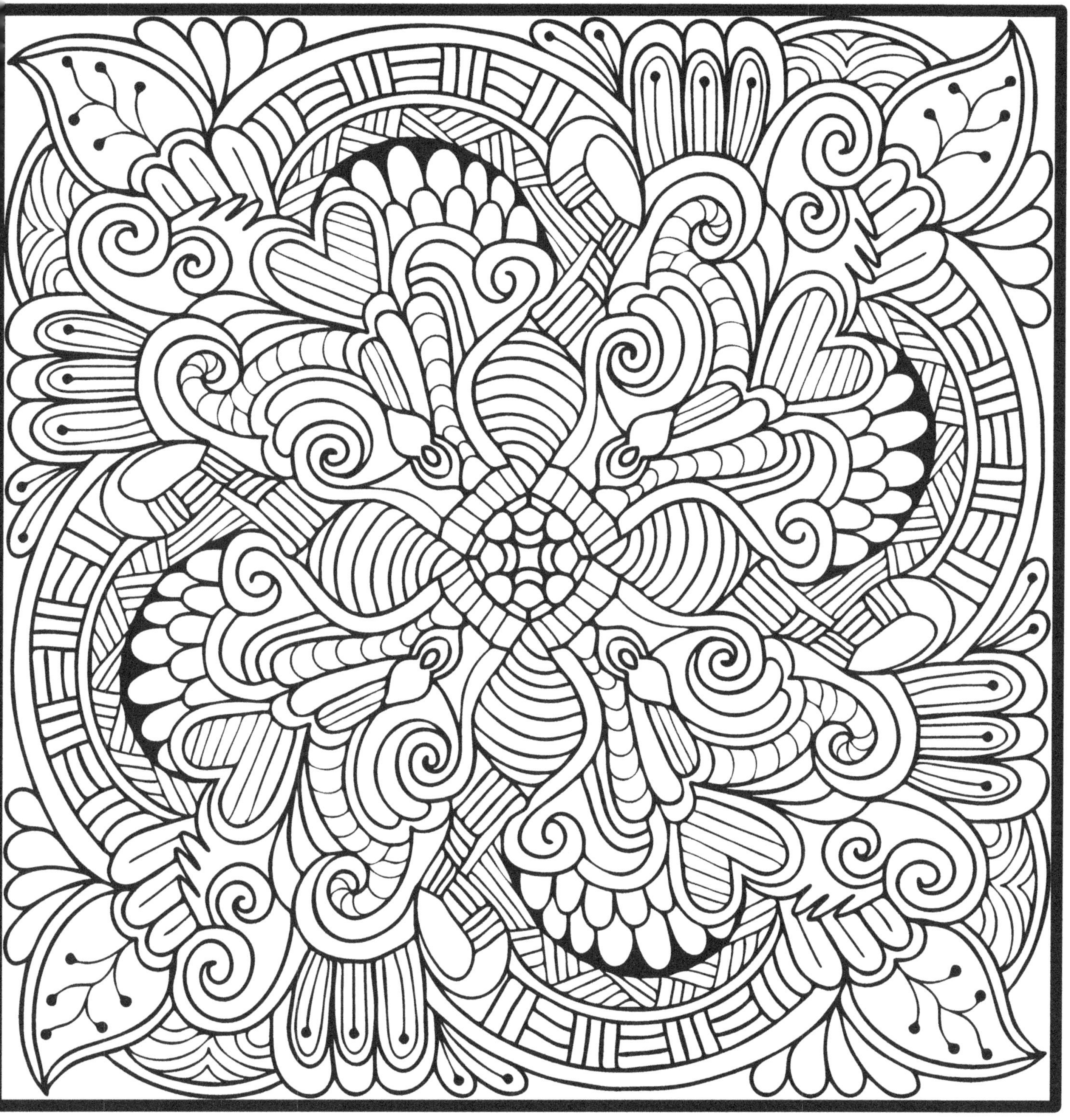

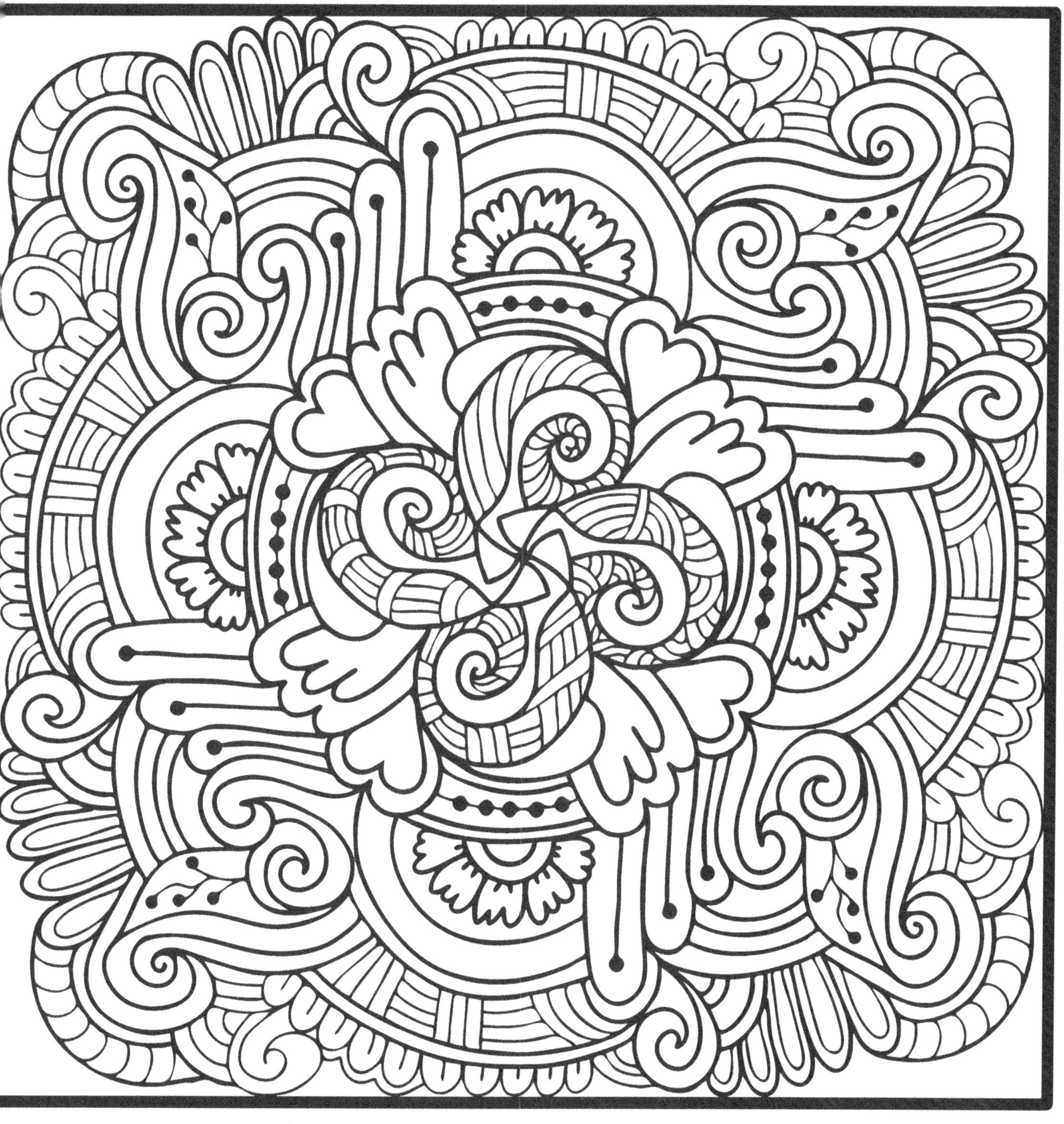

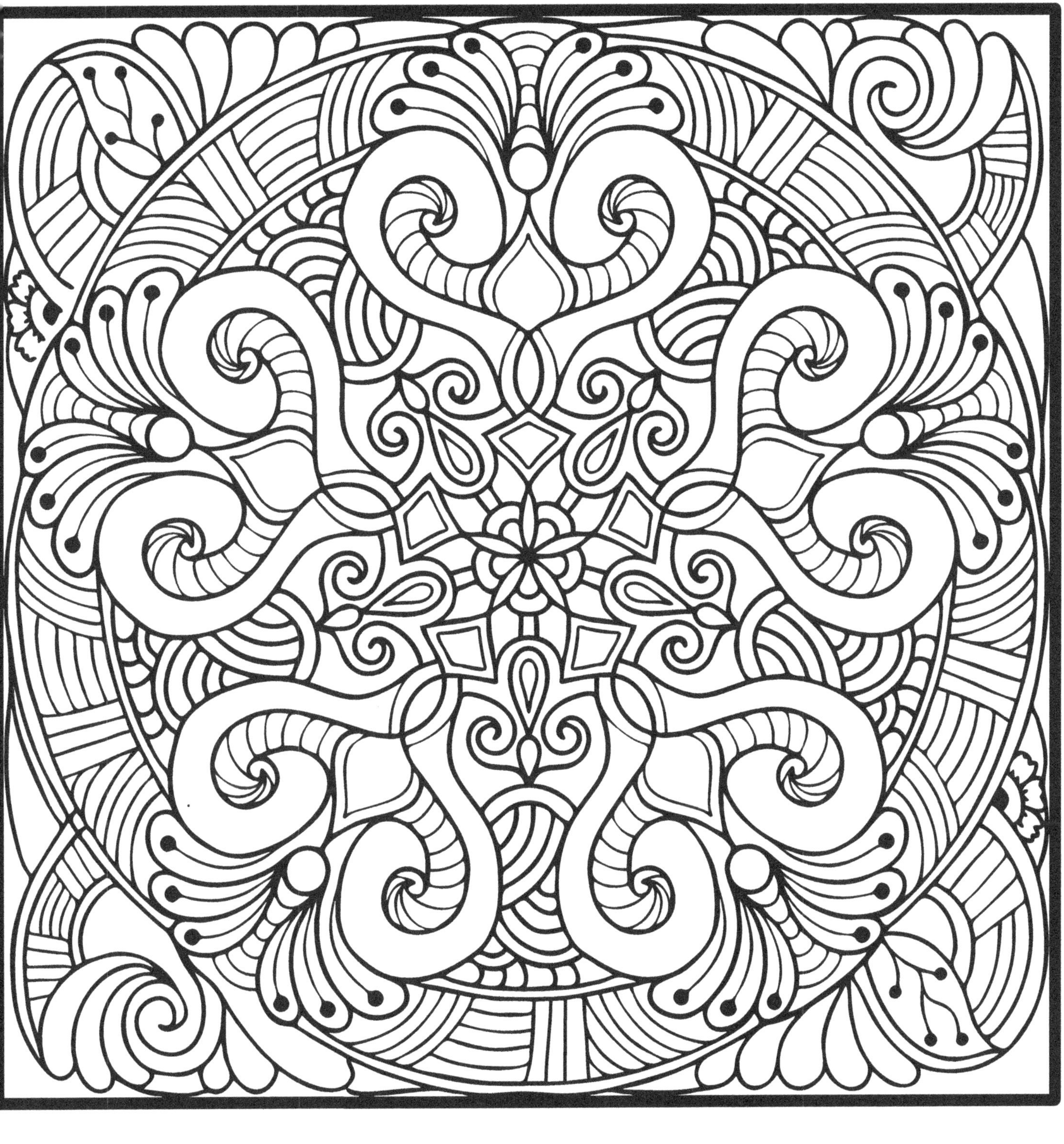

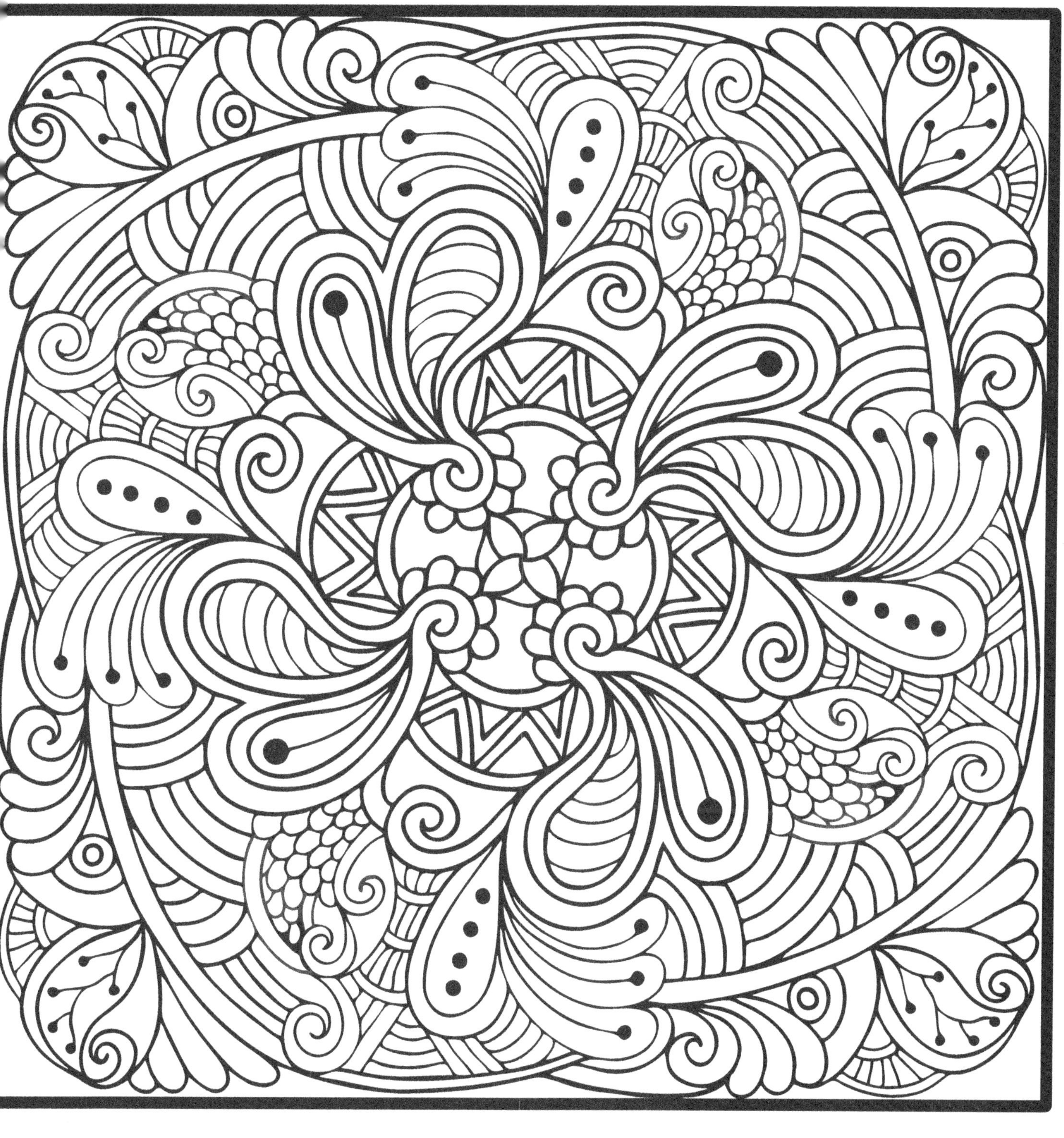

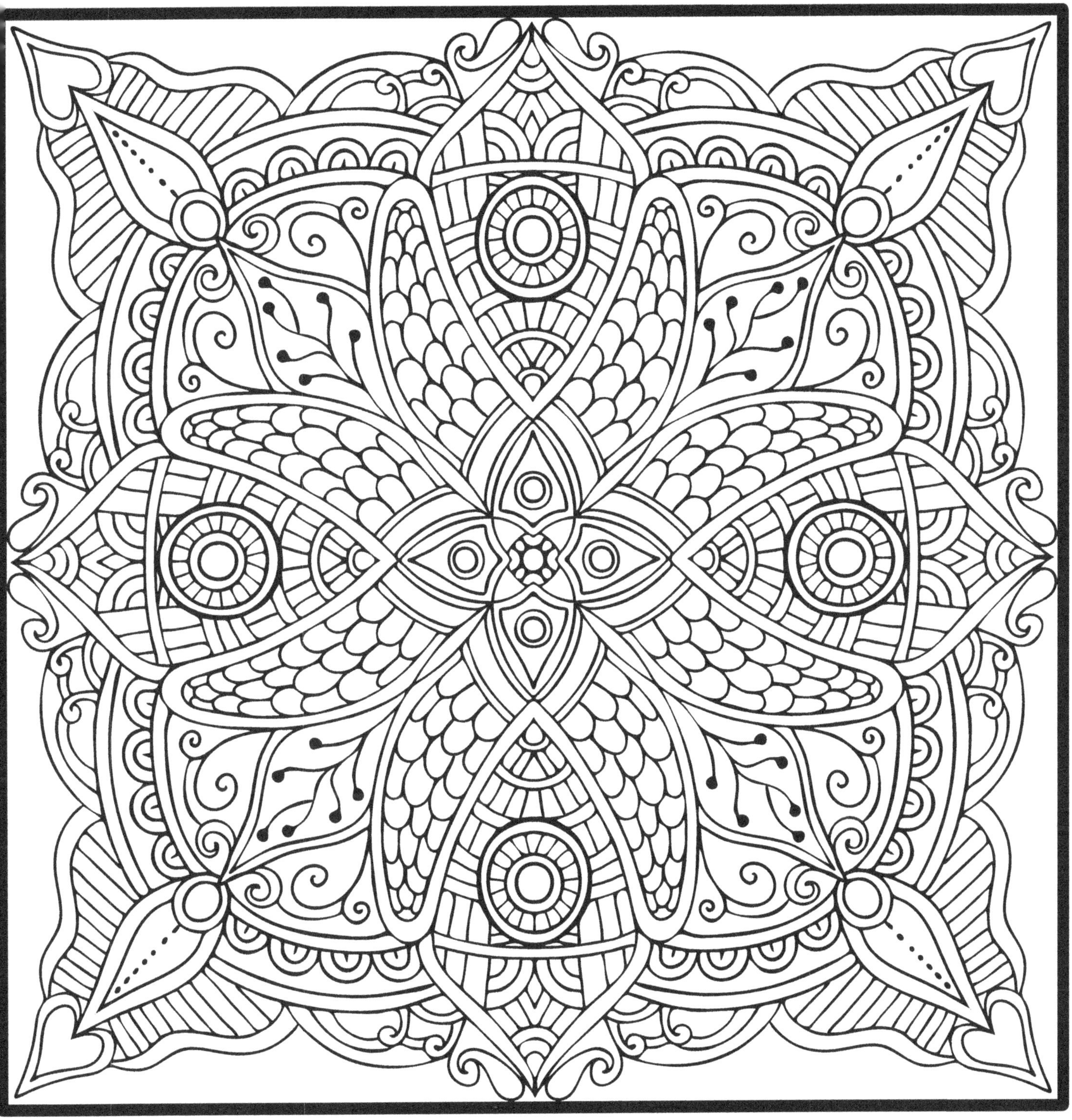

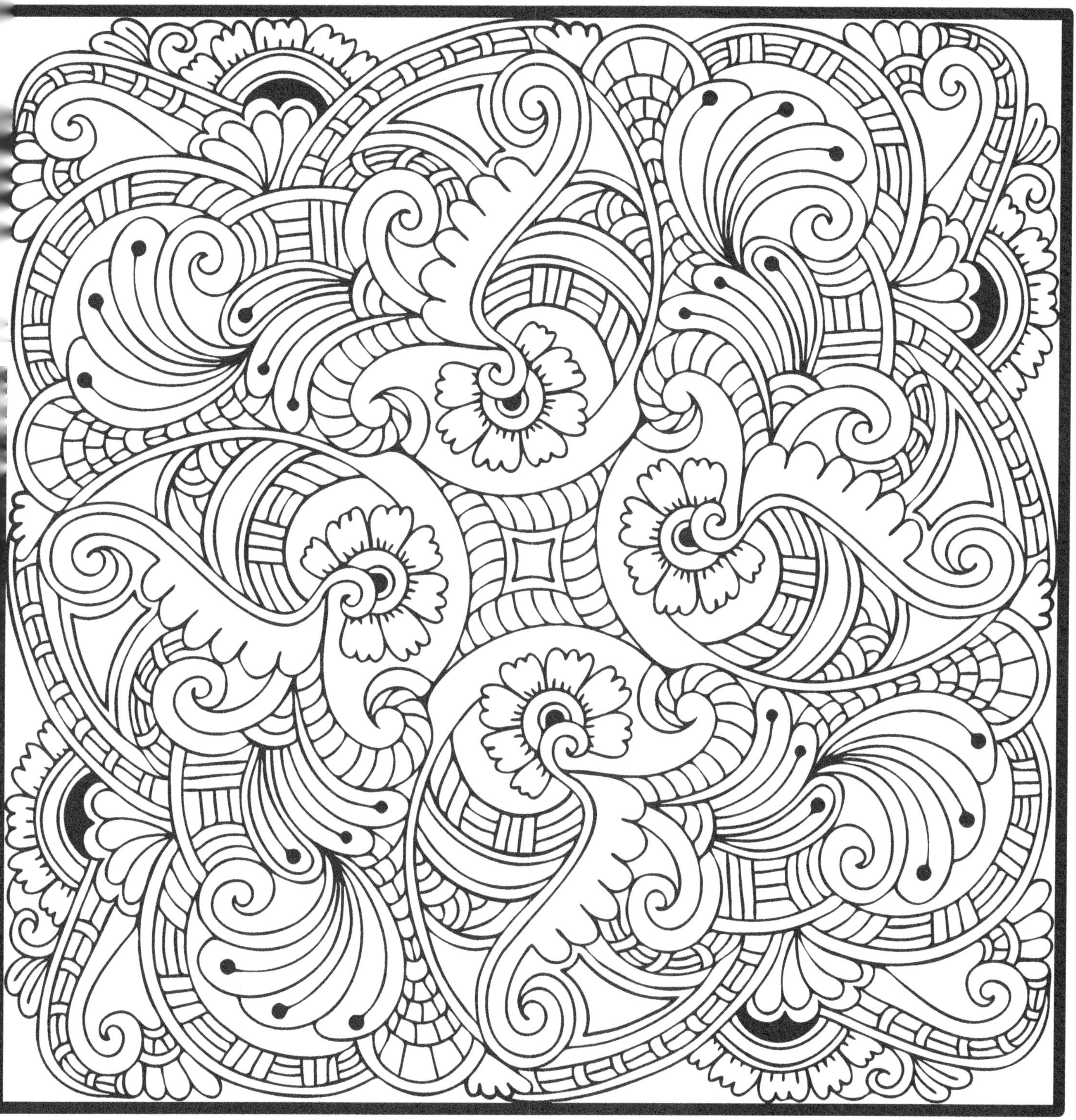

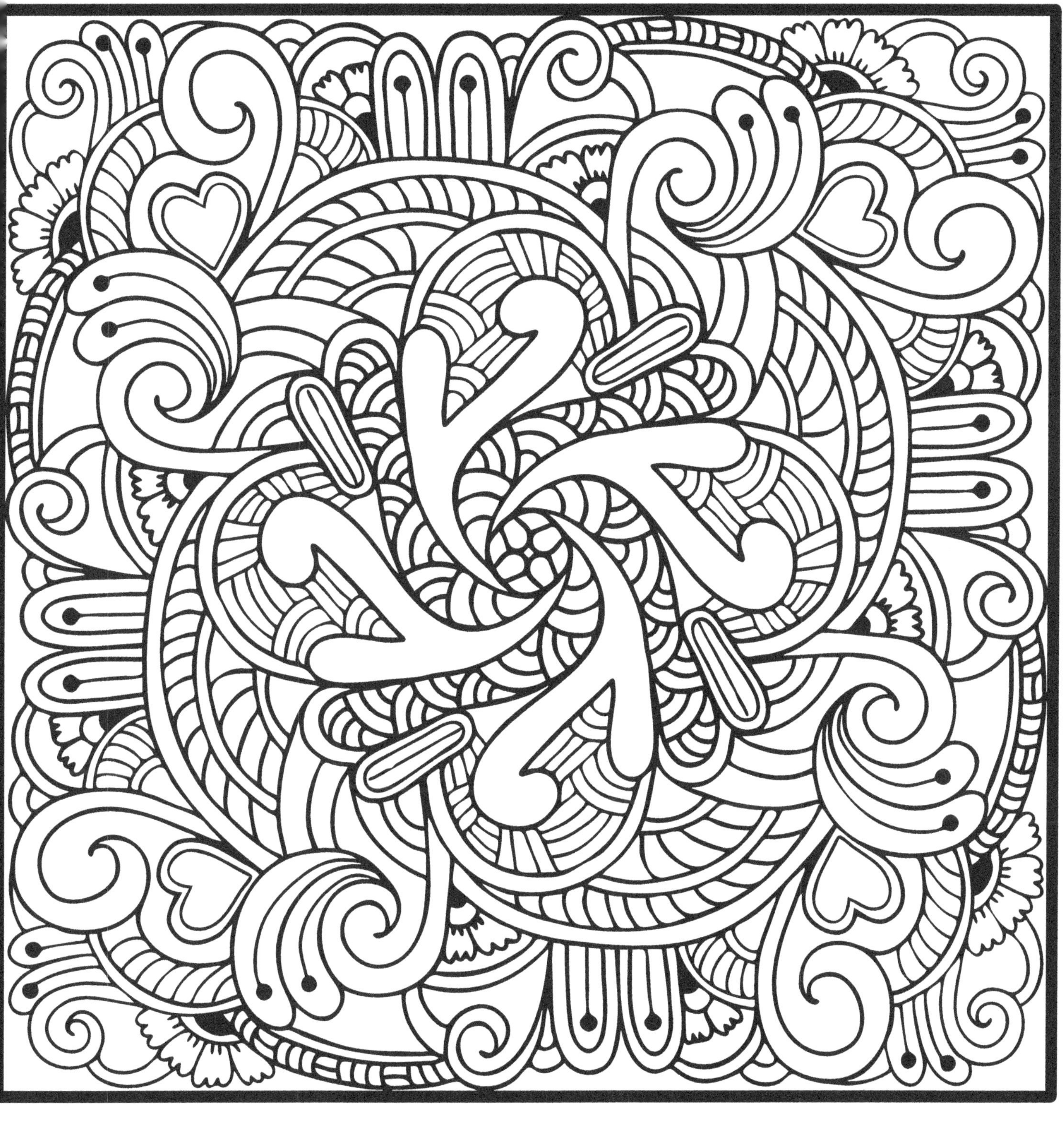

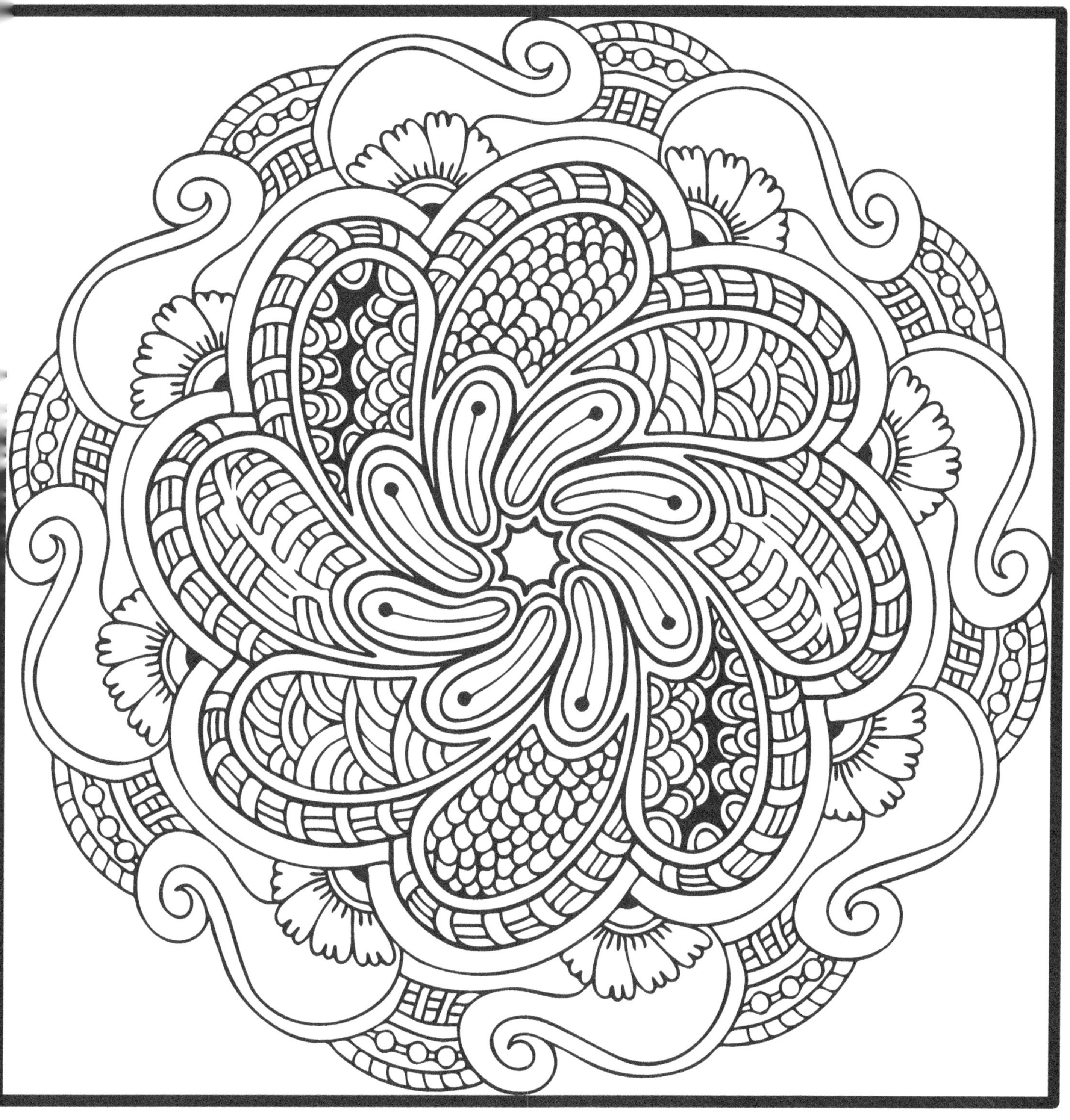

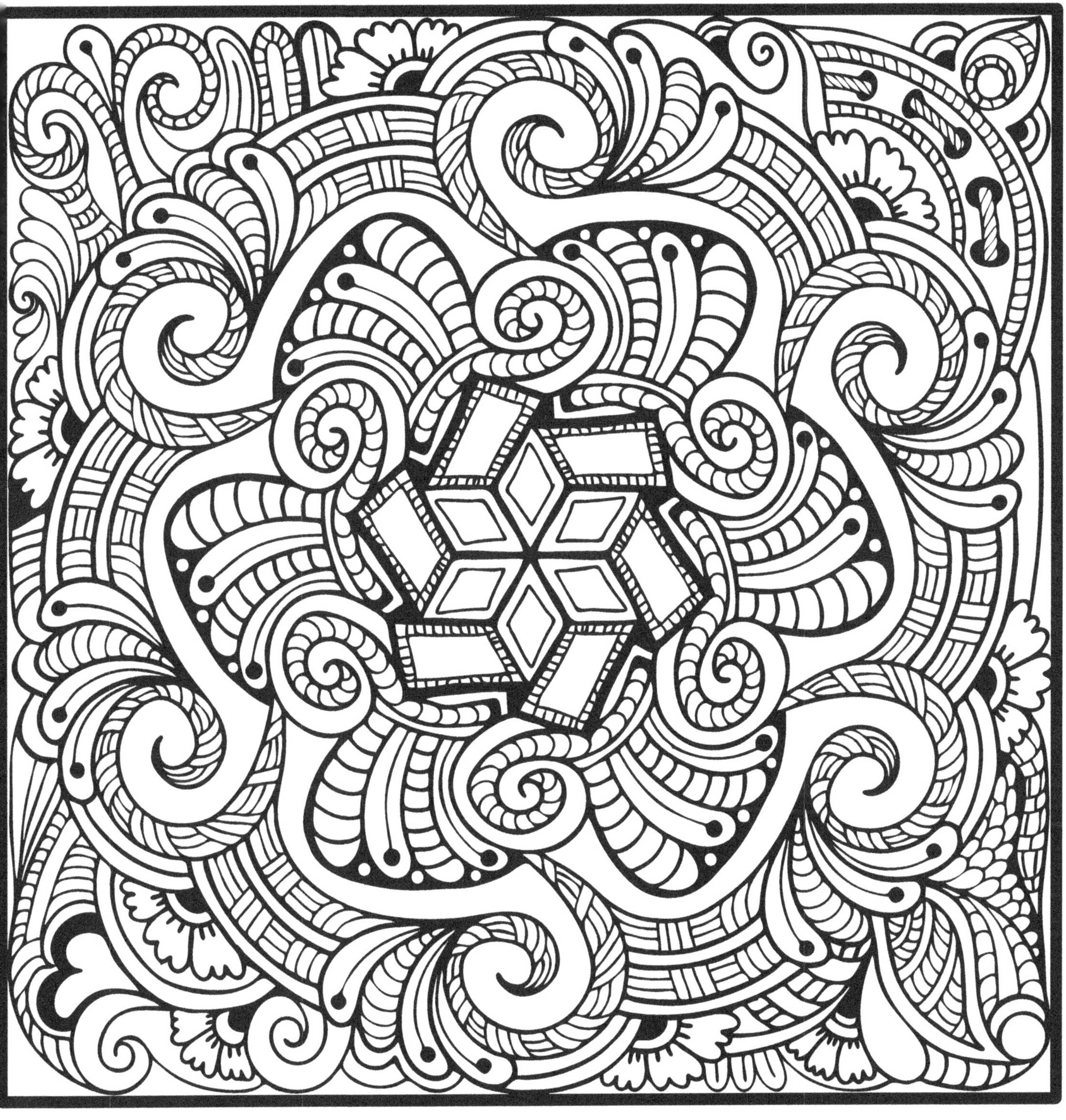

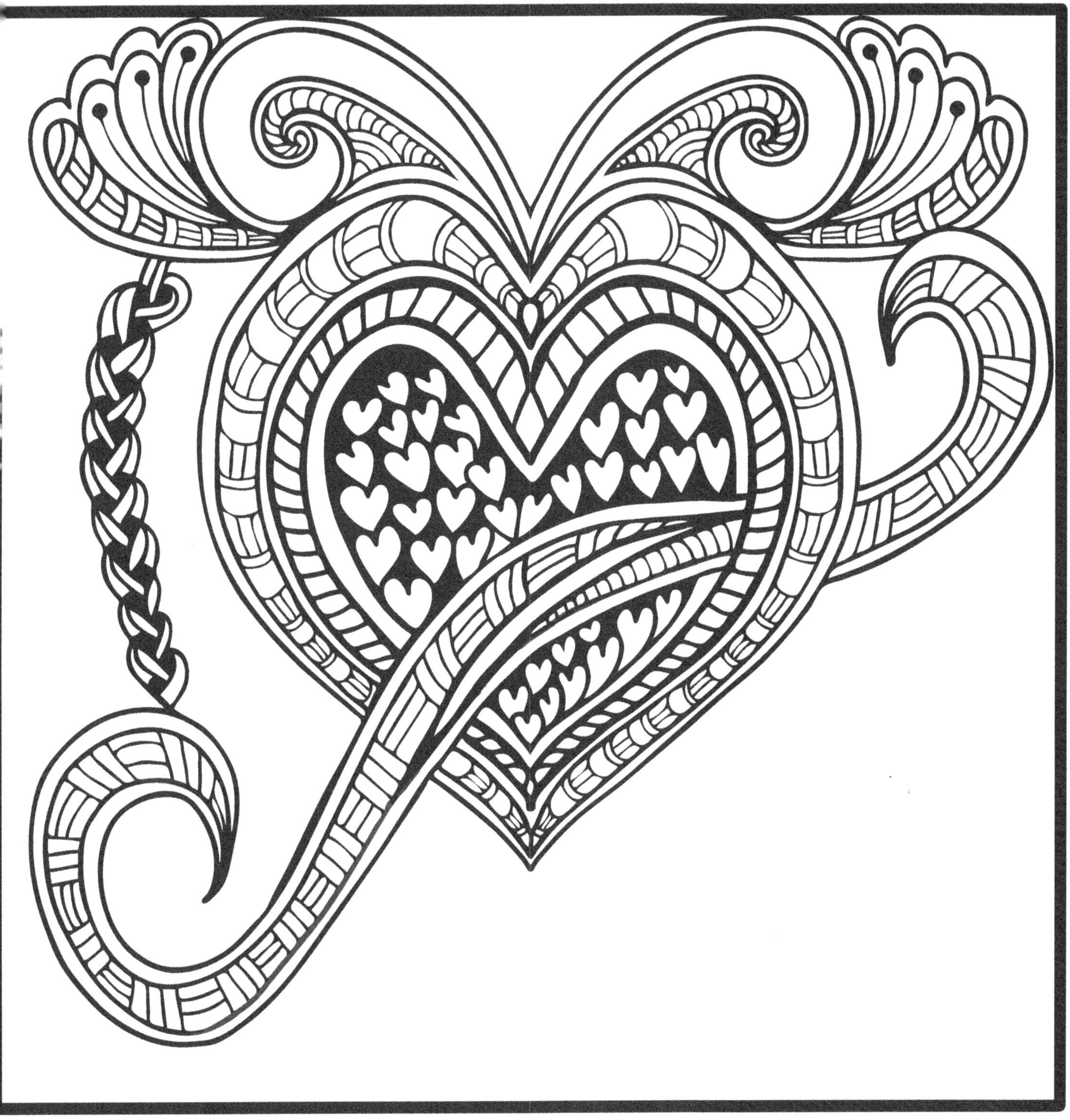

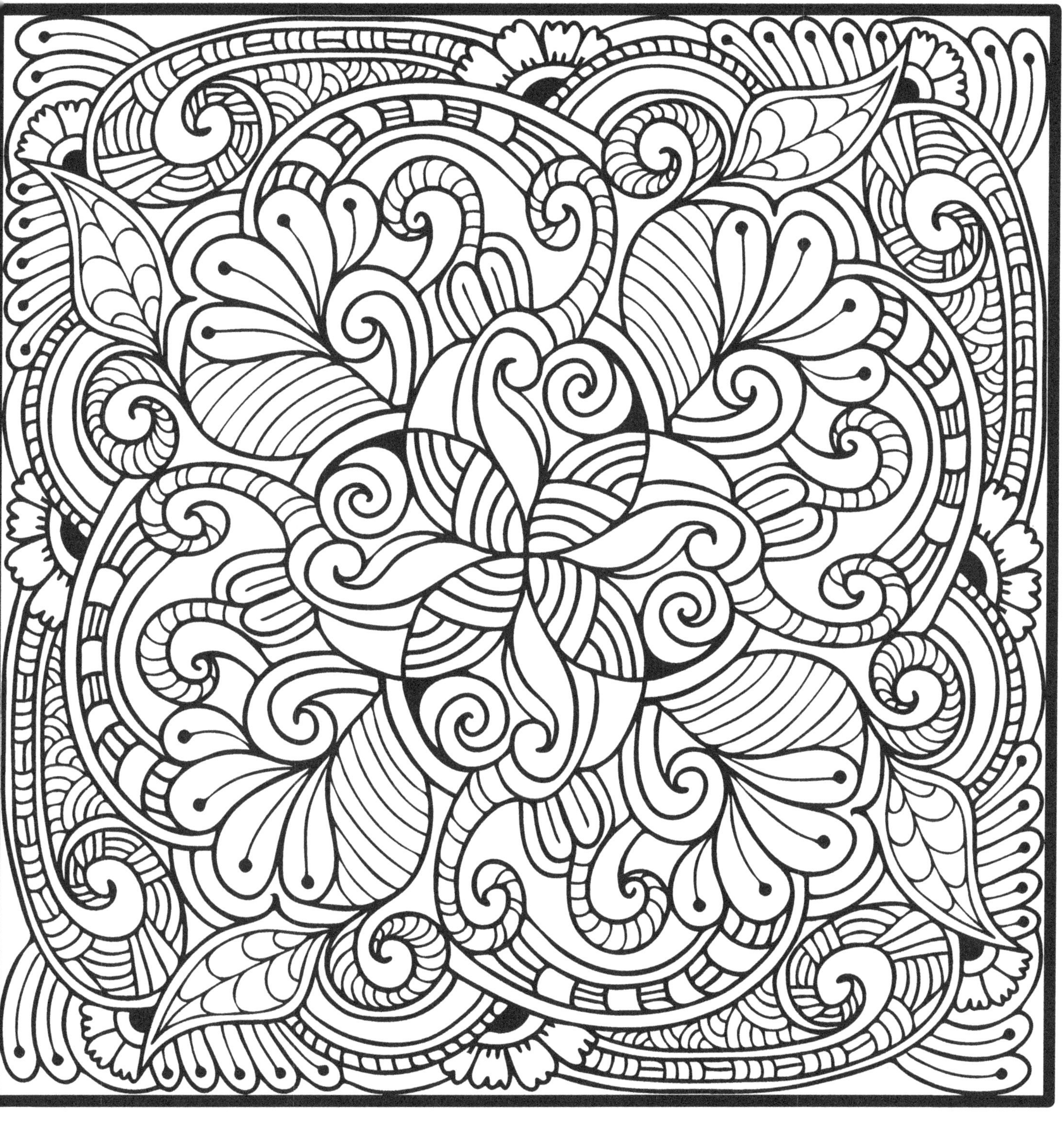

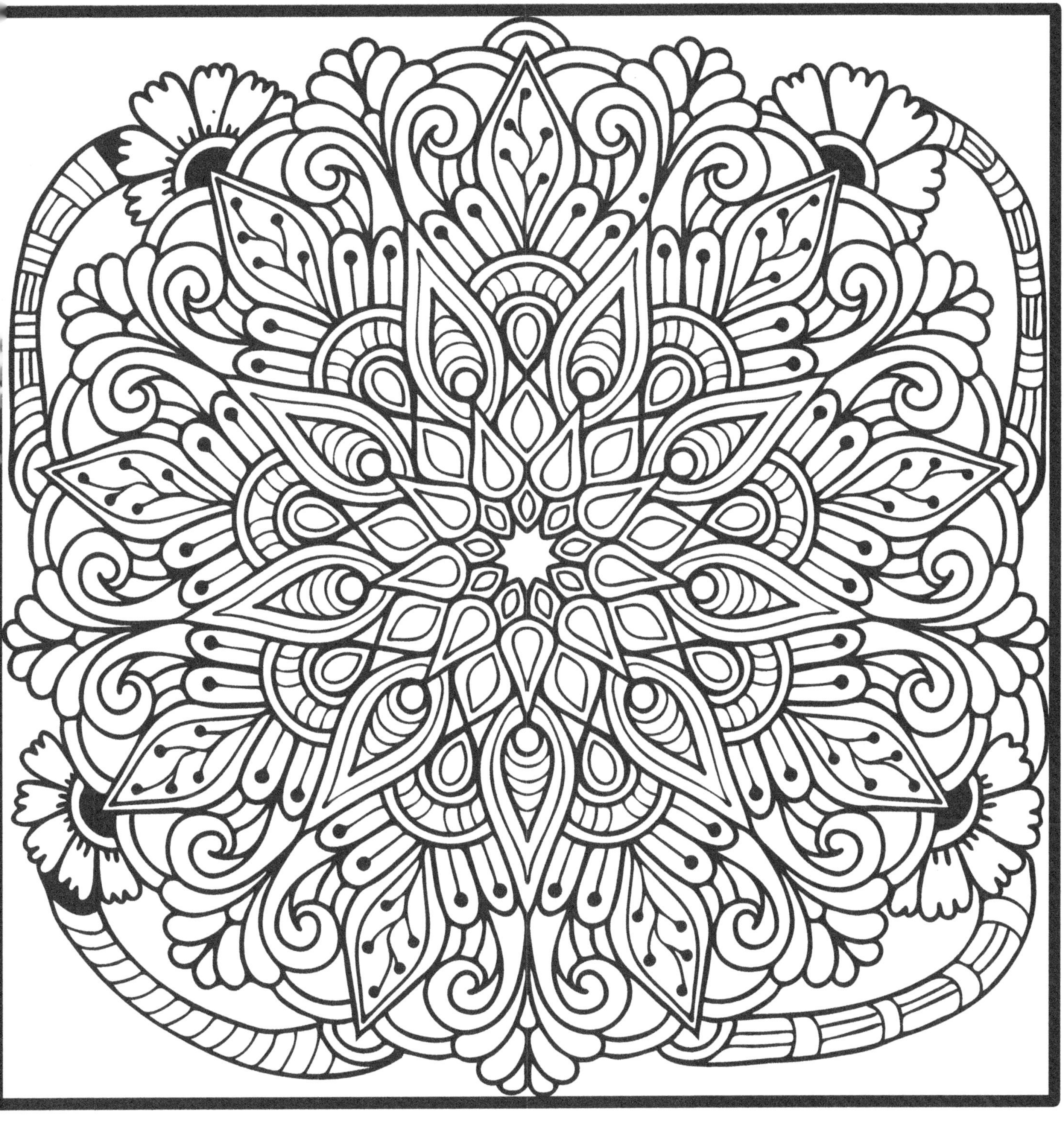

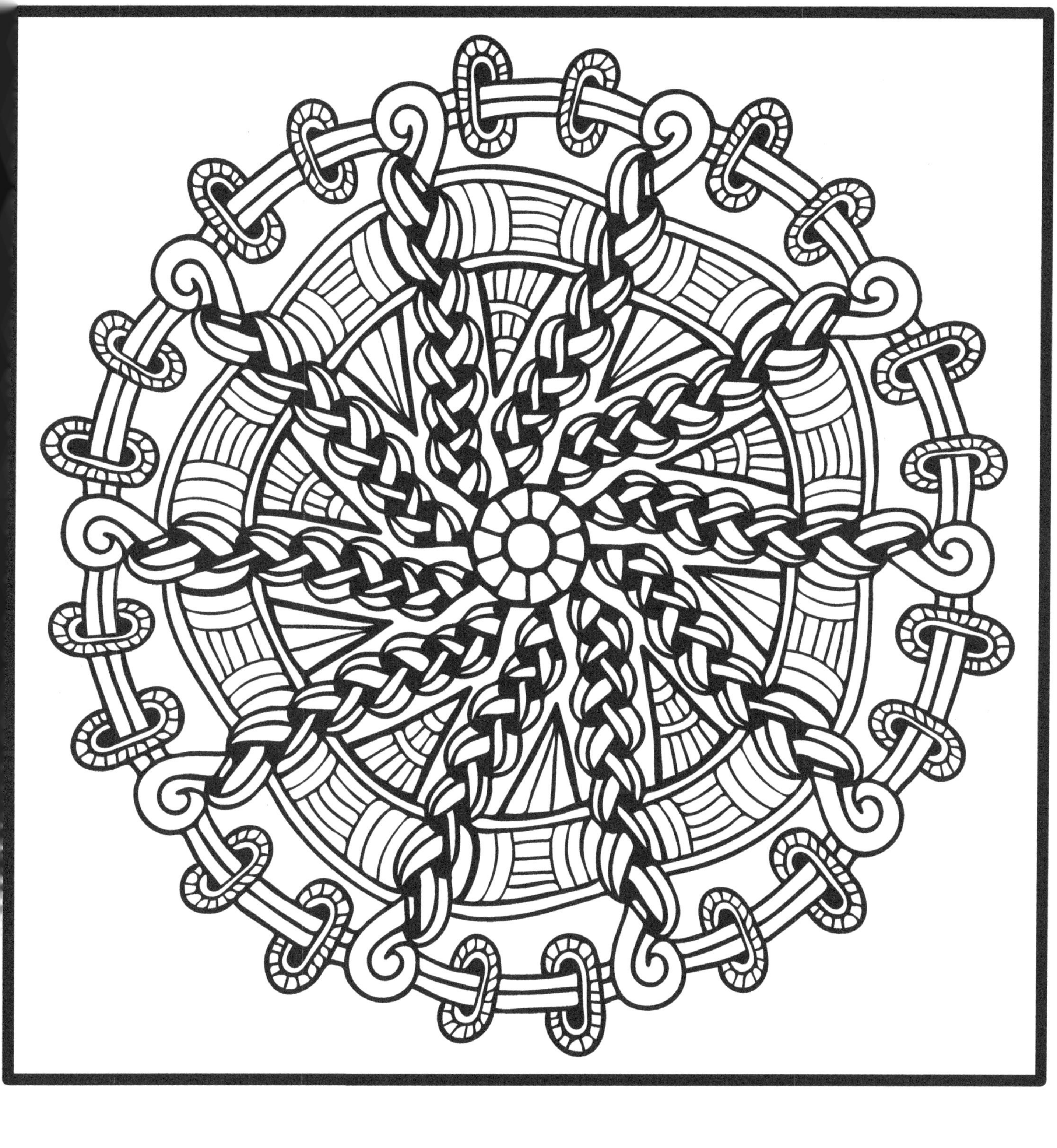

Made in the USA
Monee, IL
20 September 2024

66255373R00057